# Getting into
# The Theology of Concord

# Getting into The Theology of Concord

## A STUDY
## OF THE BOOK OF CONCORD

Robert Preus

Publishing House
St. Louis

This book is dedicated to Christ,
the Center of the Scriptures
and the Center of our Lutheran Confessions

Unless otherwise stated, quotations of the Lutheran Confessions are from *The Book of Concord*, tr. and ed. Theodore G. Tappert, © 1959, Fortress Press, Philadelphia, and used by permission.

Concordia Publishing House, St. Louis, Missouri
Copyright © 1977 Concordia Publishing House
MANUFACTURED IN THE UNITED STATES OF AMERICA

Library of Congress Cataloging in Publication Data

Preus, Robert D 1924-
    Getting into the theology of Concord.

    1. Lutheran Church. Book of Concord. I. Title.
BX8068.P73          238'.4'1          77-13425
ISBN 0-570-03567-0

3  4  5  6  7  8  9  10  11  12   CB   89 88 87 86 85 84 83 82 81 80

# CONTENTS

# Abbreviations

AC—Augsburg Confession
Ap—Apology of the Augsburg Confession
Ep—Epitome of the Formula of Concord
FC—Formula of Concord
LC—Large Catechism
SA—Smalcald Articles
SC—Small Catechism
SD—Solid Declaration of the Formula of Concord
Tr—Treatise on the Power and Primacy of the Pope

Uppercase Roman numerals following the above abbreviations denote article numbers, except in the Smalcald Articles, where they refer to parts. In the Smalcald Articles, article numbers are indicated by lowercase Roman numerals. Arabic numerals following Roman numerals identify the paragraph or paragraphs from which the citation is taken.

WA—Weimar edition of Luther's works

# Introduction

What really is a Lutheran? This is a question which has not only perplexed non-Lutherans who have observed Lutherans in our country and all over the world split into a confusing plethora of territorial churches and synods; but the question is asked, and very sincerely, by more and more Lutherans who are distressed over the disunity so apparent the world over. It is surely a valid question, and vital for millions who studied and believe Luther's Small Catechism and wish to remain faithful to its teachings and to their confirmation vow. And it is a question, ironically, which is really quite simple to answer.

This is the question I purpose to answer in this short volume, to answer for Lutheran lay people and anyone else who wishes to read it.

The answer is simple because we Lutherans for 400 years have been guided in our belief and teaching and preaching by a number of Confessions which are collected together in one volume called the *Book of Concord*.

This *Book of Concord* contains a quite divergent assortment of creeds and formal confessions which however have one thing in common, a doctrinal unity, a united commitment to the teaching of the Gospel of Christ. In this book are the ecumenical creeds, developed and written from the second to the sixth century, long before the Reformation. Included also are Luther's Small Catechism and his Large Catechism (1529), which were not originally intended to be confessions at all in the usual sense, but were written for children and ordinary adults to summarize the Christian faith and the way of salvation for them. Perhaps the most important confession included in our *Book of Concord* is the Augsburg Confession (1530), written by Philip Melanchthon and presented on behalf of the Lutheran princes of the day at a very important meeting with the emperor to testify to the world exactly what the Protestant churches in their lands taught about the

7

Christian religion and the Gospel. A year later (1531) Melanchthon wrote a defense of this great confession called the Apology of the Augsburg Confession, a very lengthy treatise in which he defends the theology of the Augsburg Confession, especially on such crucial issues of the Reformation as justification by faith, the importance of good works, the work of Christ, repentance, and the like. In 1537 Luther was asked to write a confession for a church council the pope suggested he might hold but which never came about. It was written at a little town called Smalcald and is called the Smalcald Articles. It is a bold and militant document, but at the same time exhibits Luther's great heart and concern for the Gospel and for the church, and it wins the reader by its sincerity and conviction. Later in the same year Melanchthon wrote a short Treatise on the Power and Primacy of the Pope because Luther had seemingly not said enough about this in his Smalcald Articles. This too was included in our *Book of Concord*. After Luther died, all kinds of controversies and misunderstandings broke out among the Lutherans in Germany. After years of debate and monumental attempts at settling the doctrinal issues the Formula of Concord was written in 1577. This was a joint undertaking of a great many Lutheran theologians who wanted only to settle the disputes and remain faithful to their Lutheran heritage. They were eminently successful. The Formula of Concord was signed by thousands of Lutheran pastors in the German empire; at a later date the Luthern Church in Sweden and in Hungary also signed this document. Now peace (*concordia*) was established. The Reformation and the cause of the Gospel went on, uninhibited by doctrinal controversy. In 1580 all these creeds and confessions were incorporated into the *Book of Concord,* which Lutheran pastors subscribe and to which they pledge themselves today.

In this little volume I purpose to summarize and discuss the theology of these confessions and thus answer the question: What really is a Lutheran?

Let me explain by way of introduction how I intend to do this.

1. Just as the King James Version of Scripture, one of the very first English translations, has become more difficult to read over the years because its words and terms have become obscure and unclear with the passage of time, so it is with some of the profoundest theology of the Reformation. Often the enlightened Lutheran layman today will read from

Luther's writings or the Confessions and not fully understand all he reads. Words, thought forms, and attitudes have changed since the 16th century, even though we Lutherans have tried to remain faithful to the evangelical doctrine of the Reformation. For this reason I must not merely review what is contained in the *Book of Concord*, but also clarify and explain this great theology where that seems necessary or advisable in our latter day.

2. I will need to content myself with discussing only the central teachings of the *Book of Concord* and avoid issues no longer confronting our church as directly as four centuries ago.

3. Much of the discussion will unabashedly center on the meaning of theological terms and the way they were used by Luther and the Confessions. Many common theological terms of the Reformation era are about as unfamiliar to lay people today as are modern technical medical terms. After years of teaching the Confessions to theological students and laymen, I have found that when a student or layman knows what the terms mean he knows the theology of the Lutheran Confessions.

4. Because of restrictions in the length of the volume I will be prohibited from citing the Confessions at length as much as I would desire and from sharing with the reader many of the theological gems found in these writings. I pray that this brief introduction will stimulate the reader to secure for himself the *Book of Concord* and then read it with avidity and with the blessing that thousands of clergymen have derived from it.

May I remind the reader that, although this book describes what was taught 400 years ago—and I earnestly pray that it may not seem ponderous for this reason or because it is so eminently theological throughout—still, what was taught then is precisely, or ought to be, what is believed and taught and confessed by every Lutheran pastor today. Perhaps this significant fact will prompt the reader to bear with me.

The following chapters are the result of teaching the Confessions to seminary students for 20 years, of offering scores of classes on the Confessions in congregations, and of various articles I have written in the *Lutheran Layman*, the *Lutheran Witness,* and elsewhere.

Finally, this book has been a downright pleasure to write, just as it has been my greatest joy to teach the Confessions to hundreds of men preparing for the ministry for the last 20 years. No compilation of books or statements has so adequately, so accurately, so comfortingly reflected and exhibited the Biblical Gospel as our Lutheran Confessions. *Soli Deo gloria:* to God alone the glory. I am honored to have been chosen to write this anniversary volume and doubly honored by those who read it.

# I. The Lutheran Confessions: What Are They?

## *The Spirit in Which They Were Written*

We use the word "confession" in a variety of ways today. A young man confesses his love for his fiancee. A criminal confesses to a felony. Christians confess their sins to a fellow believer or at the appropriate time in the church service. The Lutheran Confessions are something quite different from all that. They are written, formal statements with which a group of Christians or an individual declare to the world their faith, their deepest and undaunted convictions.

The Lutheran Confessions represent the result of more than 50 years of earnest endeavor by Martin Luther and his followers to give Biblical and clear expression to their religious convictions. The important word in that definition is the word "convictions." This word reveals the spirit in which the Lutheran Confessions were written, not a spirit of hesitation or doubt but of deepest confidence that Lutherans, when they were writing and subscribing the Confessions and creeds, because their content was all drawn from the Word of God, Scripture, were affirming the truth, the saving truth. Listen to what the Lutheran confessors say in the very last paragraph of the *Book of Concord* (FC SD, XII, 40), a statement that describes their assurance and their doctrinal certainty:

> Therefore, in the presence of God and of all Christendom among both our contemporaries and our posterity, we wish to have testified that the present explanation of all the foregoing controverted articles here explained, and none other, is our teaching, belief, and confession in which by God's grace we shall appear with intrepid hearts before the judgment seat of Jesus Christ and for which we shall give an account. Nor shall we speak or write anything, privately or publicly, contrary to this confession, but we intend through God's grace to abide by it.

Here we observe that those who wrote and signed the Lutheran Confessions were not merely settling controversies, or expressing opinions, or devising new and clever doctrinal formulations. They were confessing their faith and expressing their determination never to depart from that confession. They take their stand as in the presence of God and stake their very salvation on the doctrine they confess. So confident are they of their position, so certain of their doctrine, that they dare bind not only themselves but also their posterity to it. And in another place they show their willingness to submit themselves not only to the content but to the very phrases of their confession: "We have determined not to depart even a finger's breadth either from the subjects themselves, or from the phrases which are found in [the Confessions]" (Preface of the *Book of Concord,* quoted from *Concordia Triglotta* [St. Louis: Concordia, 1921], p. 23).

I am sure that such a profession seems like an impossible anachronism today, a mark of inflexible pride which can no longer be respected or emulated by enlightened people. But certainly with such expressions of certainty the Confessions have captured the spirit of Christ and the New Testament. Our Lord taught with authority and promised His disciples that they would "know the truth." And how often does the inspired apostle Paul dogmatically affirm, "I know," "I speak the truth," "I am persuaded"!

The Lutheran confessors are convinced that Christians, basing their doctrine on Scripture and the promises of God, can be certain of their salvation and can formulate and confess true statements about God and all the articles of the Christian faith. It is this spirit in which all our Confessions were written and in which they so eloquently give witness to the Gospel of Christ.

### The Importance of Doctrine

According to the Lutheran Confessions, true doctrine, i. e., correct teaching about God and His activity toward us, is not some remote possibilty but a marvelous fact, the result of God's grace; and this doctrine is demonstrated in the Confessions themselves. Those who wrote our Confessions were convinced of this (FC SD, Rule and Norm, 13); but more than that, they were persuaded that true doctrine, theology (which means language about God), is of inestimable importance to the church and to individual Christians. Why?

1. It is first and foremost by pure doctrine that we honor God and hallow His name, as we pray in the First Petition of the Small Catechism. "For," Luther says, "there is nothing he would rather hear than to have his glory and praise exalted above everything and his Word taught in its purity and cherished and treasured" (LC, III, 48).

2. It is by agreement in the pure doctrine that permanent concord and harmony can be achieved in the church. "In order to preserve the pure doctrine and to maintain a thorough, lasting, and God-pleasing concord within the church, it is essential not only to present the true and wholesome doctrine correctly, but also to accuse the adversaries who teach otherwise (I Tim. 3:9; Titus 1:9; II Tim. 2:24; 3:16)" (FC SD, Rule and Norm, 14).

3. Doctrine is important to Lutherans because they believe that Christian doctrine is not a human fabrication but originates in God. It is God's revealed teaching about Himself and all He has done for us in Christ. Therefore Luther says confidently and joyfully: "The doctrine is not ours but God's" (WA, 17 II, 233). And he will risk everything for the doctrine, for to compromise would do harm to God and to all the world. Luther's spirit is echoed throughout our Confessions as they affirm that their doctrine is "drawn from and conformed to the Word of God" (FC SD, Rule and Norm, 5, 10).

4. Pure Christian doctrine is important for our Lutheran Confessions because it brings eternal salvation. It "alone is our guide to salvation" (Preface to the *Book of Concord, Concordia Triglotta,* p. 11). For this reason our Confessions call it "heavenly doctrine" and they never fail to show and apply this saving aim of evangelical doctrine.

This emphasis on the importance of Christian doctrine is often not understood or appreciated in our day of relativism and indifference.

How often do modern church leaders declaim that the church will never achieve purity of doctrine; nor is it necessary! Therefore we should concentrate our efforts toward ministry to people in their needs. The longest article in our Confessions deals with good works and ministry to people in their needs (Ap, IV, 122-400) and insistently admonishes the church to follow such an enterprise. But this does not make doctrine less important! Today when people are leaving the church in droves and abandoning the faith, we must keep our priorities straight. Luther says:

> The great difference between doctrine and life is obvious, even as the difference between heaven and earth. Life may be unclean, sinful, and inconsistent; but doctrine must be pure, holy, sound, unchanging . . . not a tittle or letter may be omitted, however much life may fail to meet the requirements of doctrine. This is so because doctrine is God's Word, and God's truth alone, whereas life is partly our own doing. . . . God will have patience with man's moral failings and imperfections and forgive them. But He cannot, will not, and shall not tolerate a man's altering or abolishing doctrine itself. For doctrine involves His exalted, divine Majesty itself (WA, 30 III, 343 f.)

Strong words! But this is the spirit of confessional Lutheranism.

Again theologians remind us today that what matters for the Christian is his faith relation to Christ: Faith is directed toward Christ and not a body of doctrine. Of course! And how often do our Confessions stress just this point! But the Christ in whom we believe and live and hope is not a phantom or myth, but the very Son of God who became a man, who really lived and suffered and died as our Substitute, and who rose again for our justification. In short, He is the Christ of whom we can speak meaningfully and cognitively; and the minute we begin to speak about Him and confess Him, we are speaking doctrine.

Again we are told that we are saved by Christ, not by pure doctrine. True! But does this make pure doctrine unimportant? We are not saved by good works or social concern either. But does that make social concern and works of love of no account? No, pure doctrine has its function. It enables us to glorify God with our lips, to teach and proclaim a pure and saving Gospel and not a false gospel, to bring poor sinners to know their true condition and to know God as He is, a wonderful and gracious Savior, and not to flounder seeking and chasing phantoms.

Let us take our Confessions seriously when they see pure doctrine as a wonderful gift and instrument for glorifying God and building His church. This was Paul's conviction: "Take heed unto thyself, and unto the doctrine; continue in them; for in doing this thou shalt both save thyself and them that hear thee" (1 Tim. 4:16).

14

Lutherans have always held that creeds and confessions are necessary for the well-being of the church. Just as Christ's church and all Christians are called upon to confess their faith (Matt. 10:32; Rom. 10:9; 1 Peter 3:15; 1 John 4:2), so the church, if it is to continue to proclaim the pure Gospel in season and out of season, must for many reasons construct formal and permanent symbols and confessions and require pastors and teachers to subscribe these confessions. It is impossible for the church to be a nonconfessional church, just as impossible as to be a nonconfessing church. And so today and ever since the Reformation Lutheran churches over the world have required their pastors to subscribe the Lutheran Confessions.

What does this mean? With her confessions the church is speaking to the world, but also to God, who has spoken to her in His Word—speaking to Him in total commitment, speaking to Him by an unequivocal, unconditional response in the spirit of, "We believe, teach, and confess" (FC Ep, Rule and Norm, 1). This response is Scriptural, taken from Scripture itself. How often do we read in our Confessions that the teaching presented is "grounded in God's Word"! And so the Confessions are no more than a kind of "comprehensive summary, rule, and norm," grounded in the Word of God, "according to which all doctrines should be judged and the errors which intruded should be explained and decided in a Christian way" (FC Ep, Heading). This would be an unbelievably arrogant position to take, were it not for the fact that all the doctrine of our Confessions is diligently and faithfully drawn from Scripture.

And so when the Lutheran pastor subscribes the Lutheran Confessions (and the confirmand or layman confesses his belief in the Catechism [LC, Preface, 19]), this is a primary way in which he willingly and joyfully and without reservation or qualification confesses his faith and proclaims to the world what his belief and doctrine and confession really are. Dr. C. F. W. Walther, the father of the Missouri Synod, long ago explained the meaning of confessional subscription, and his words are as cogent today as when they were first written:

An unconditional subscription is the solemn declaration which the individual who wants to serve the church makes under oath (1) that he accepts the *doctrinal content* of our Symbolical Books, because he recognizes the fact that it is in full agreement with Scripture and does not militate against Scripture in any point, whether that point be of major or minor importance; (2) that he therefore heartily believes in this divine truth and is determined to preach this doctrine. . . . Whether the subject be dealt with expressly or only incidentally, an unconditional subscription refers to the whole content of the Symbols and does not allow the subscriber to make any mental reservation in any point. Nor will he exclude such doctrines as are discussed incidentally in support of other doctrines, because the fact that they are so stamps them as irrevocable articles of faith and demands their joyful acceptance by everyone who subscribes the Symbols.

This is precisely how the Confessions themselves understand subscription (FC Ep, Rule and Norm, 3, 5, 6; SD, Rule and Norm, 1, 2, 5).

Needless to say, confessional subscription in the nature of the case is binding and unconditional. A subscription with qualifications or reservations is a contradiction in terms and dishonest.

Today many Lutherans claim that such an unconditional subscription is legalistic. Sometimes they assert that such a position is pompous and not even honest.

We might respond: What can possibly be wrong about confessing our faith freely and taking our confession seriously? For it is the freest and most joyful act in the world for those of us who have searched these great confessional writings and found them to be Scriptural and evangelical to subscribe them. Of course, to force or bribe or wheedle a person into subscribing them would be an awful sin and a denial of what our Confessions are, namely symbols, standards around which Christians rally willingly and joyfully in all their Christian freedom.

### Confessions Are the Voice of the Church

When I was a boy my father told me a curious story about an occurrence in the 19th century. During the controversy among Lutherans concerning predestination, the old Norwegian Synod sided with the Missouri Synod. One member of the Norwegian Synod demurred vehemently and in his consternation said, "I am the Norwegian Synod." That, of course, was an absurdity, just as it would be absurd for me to claim, "I am the church." The church, as we shall see,

16

according to our Confessions is the total of all believers in Christ.

So it is, in a similar sense, with the Confessions. They do not belong to Luther or Melanchthon or those who, sometimes after great struggles, wrote them. They belong to those for whom they were written, the church. Princes subscribed the Augsburg Confession on behalf of their churches. Luther's catechisms were finally subscribed because the lay people had already accepted them. Thousands of clergy subscribed the entire *Book of Concord,* and the only reason the laity did not do so was the length of the book.

All this suggests two things. First, that every Lutheran ought to be concerned with what is rightfully his and ought to agree with the doctrine of the Confessions. But it suggests also that, if the Confessions really belong to the entire church, then everyone in the church ought to be united in the evangelical doctrine of the Confessions. That was the case when the *Book of Concord* was compiled in 1580, and it ought to be the case today.

### Doctrinal Unanimity, a Blessing to the Church

The Church of the Reformation after the death of Luther in one respect resembled the congregation at Corinth in the first century: It was a church highly endowed with the gifts of the Spirit, but at the same time tragically confused and divided. To the Corinthian congregation Paul wrote: "Now I beseech you, brethren, by the name of our Lord Jesus Christ, that ye all speak the same thing, and that there be no divisions among you; but that ye be perfectly joined together in the same mind and in the same judgment" (1 Cor. 1:10). Paul had no quarrel with the diversity of spiritual gifts he found in that congregation; he rejoiced in all that, provided it did not polarize the church. But there is only one Christ, he says, who is undivided; one Gospel; and all Christians are to be of the same mind and judgment, united in their faith and doctrine.

The Church of the Reformation took Paul's admonition seriously when after Luther's death doctrinal controversies arose and threatened to destroy its unity in the Gospel. The Lutheran churches recognized that the unity of the Spirit which Paul stressed could only be manifested when there was unanimity "in doctrine and in all its articles and . . . the right use of the holy sacraments" (FC SD, X, 31). Their program for unity and concord in a troubled church went as follows: "The primary requirement for basic and permanent concord within the church is a summary formula and pattern, *unanimously approved,* in which the summarized doctrine commonly confessed by the churches of the pure Christian religion is drawn together out of the Word of God" (FC SD, Rule and Norm, 1).

What a remarkable statement! Here is not the cynical despairing of the possibility of doctrinal unity, so common to our relativistic age! not the sneering rejection of doctrinal unanimity as something inimical to man's freedom and autonomy. No, here is a statement of confidence in the unifying power of the Word and Spirit of God. These old Lutherans were convinced that doctrinal controversies were an offense and doctrinal aberrations pernicious to believers and unbelievers alike. "The opinions of the erring party cannot be tolerated in the church of God," they said, "much less be excused and defended" (FC SD, Intro., 9). But at the same time they maintained with Paul-like optimism that unity in doctrine and all its articles was not a remote possibility, not an impossible goal at the end of a rainbow, but a wonderful blessing that could be achieved by the church which would bow to the Word of God and allow the Spirit to rule in all its life.

And so the Lutheran confessors dare to produce a confession which all are asked to sign and which represents the unanimous declaration of all. They pledge themselves to the *Book of Concord* and confess: "We have from our hearts and with our mouths declared *in mutual agreement* that we shall neither prepare nor accept a different or a new confession of our faith. Rather, we pledge ourselves again to those public and well-known symbols or common confessions which have at all times and in all places been accepted in all the churches of the Augsburg Confession" (FC SD, Rule and Norm, 2). And they dare to maintain: "All doctrines should conform to the standards [the Lutheran Confessions] set forth above. Whatever is contrary to them should be rejected and condemned as opposed to the *unanimous* declaration of our faith" (FC Ep, Rule and Norm, 6). Do such statements reveal pride, cocksureness, narrowness? Not at all! But Pauline, Spirit-led confidence and optimism.

If only we could recapture this spirit today! Openness is an in-word today. And a "wholesome latitude" in doctrine is considered by many Lutherans to be a positive blessing to the church. Not many years ago a Lutheran synod actually stated (but later modified, thank goodness): "We are firmly convinced that it is neither necessary nor possible to agree in all non-fundamental doctrines." But where do the Scriptures or our Confessions say such a thing? Where are we ever told that we Christians need not agree on what Scripture affirms? Yes, let us be open to people's desires and needs, to their diversity of gifts and opinions. But not to error. Let us rather give heed to Paul's words and speak the same thing and be perfectly joined together in the same mind and judgment. Let us face up to doctrinal differences wherever they arise and impinge upon our unity. And let us seek and treasure the doctrinal unanimity of which our Confessions speak. Then we may call ourselves Lutherans.

# II. The Lutheran Confessions and the Bible

## Scripture Is Divinely Authoritative

The average Lutheran layman today may not know any Latin, but he probably knows what the phrase *sola Scriptura* (Scripture alone) means. It means that we Lutherans base our theology solely on the Scriptures of God and nothing else, not tradition, not human speculation, not modern scholarship, not our experiences or feelings or anything else. *Sola Scriptura* is a watchword, a guide for action, for every true Lutheran, pastor or layman.

This was the position and practice of Luther and our Lutheran Confessions. "The Word of God is and should remain the sole rule and norm of all doctrine" (FC SD, Rule and Norm, 9). "We pledge ourselves to the prophetic and apostolic writings of the Old and New Testaments as the pure and clear fountain of Israel, which is the only true norm according to which all teachers and teachings are to be judged" (FC SD, Rule and Norm, 3). This is the spirit in which our great Lutheran Confessions speak. Everything we need to believe and do as Christians is told us in the Scriptures. Just as our Lord Jesus was a man of one Book and drew all His teaching from that one divine source and submitted Himself to it utterly in all He said and did, so we too who are His disciples today place ourselves joyfully under that prophetic and apostolic Word. And with our Lutheran Confessions we say: "No human being's writings dare be put on a par with it, but . . . everything must be subjected to it" (FC SD, Rule and Norm, 9).

What persuades us as Christians to render such an exalted place to the Scriptures in our lives and teachings? It is the marvelous content of Scripture, which is the Gospel—as Luther said, "Christ is involved in Scripture through and through, like the body in its clothes" (WA, 12, 418). And it is the Spirit of Christ who witnesses in our hearts that as Scripture speaks judgment and grace it proclaims God's judgment and grace to all men. We believe in the absolute authority of Scripture because Christ accepted the absolute authority of the prophetic Word of the Old Testament and because He guaranteed the absolute authority of the apostolic Word of the New Testament by His promise of the Holy Spirit to His apostles.

Why is Scripture authoritative? Edmund Schlink of Heidelberg answers: "Because God saves through the Word proclaimed by it." But this is no answer to the question and confuses the issue. God saves also through the Word proclaimed in hymns and sermons and Christian literature. No, Scripture is authoritative because it is God's Word. How often do our Confessions contrast God's Word in Scripture to any human being's writings and insist that all our doctrine be drawn "out of God's Word" (FC SD, Rule and Norm, 3, 4, 5, 9, 10, 16; Ep, 1, 7, 8)! And Luther says: "The Word of God shall establish articles of faith and no one else, not even an angel" (SA, II, ii, 15). In contrast to all other writings and human authorities, God's Word carries with it God's authority.

And this authority is absolute and final. What Scripture asserts God asserts, what it commands He commands, what it promises God promises! Because our Lutheran Confessions believe in such infallible authority, they cite the Scriptures hundreds of times and regard Scripture's answers to the great problems and issues of their day as God's answers.

Today such a conviction regarding Biblical authority is rejected by many theologians. The Bible cannot carry divine authority with it, because it is not the very Word of God, they say. Although it may somehow "convey" or "contain" or "become" the Word of God, it must be read like any other human book. This is exactly the posture taken by many who use the "historical-critical method" (also called "higher criticism"), employed within the church by some scholars for about 200 years, since the time of Rationalism and the Enlightenment in Europe.

It is quite clear that such modern views—which were shared by unbelievers in the early centuries of church history—are not compatible with the position of Luther and our Confessions. The approach of higher criticism is likely to result in questioning, again and again, the evangelical doctrine which is drawn from the right reading of the Sacred Scriptures. Today, after 400 years, we need have no doubt concerning the divine authority of Scripture and therefore of our Gospel message drawn from it. And today Scripture still authenticates itself as the only source of our knowledge of God and of His grace.

### Threefold Tier of Authority in the Church

Now that we have talked about the authority of our Confessions and creeds as norms for teaching in the church and also about the authority of Scripture, the reader may be a bit confused. Are there, then, levels of authority? Yes. Precisely. Specifically there is a threefold tier of authority in the church, according to our Confessions.

1. "The prophetic and apostolic writings of the Old and New Testaments" are "the pure and clear fountain of Israel, which is the only true norm according to which all teachers and teachings are to be judged and evaluated" (FC SD, Rule and Norm, 3). That statement means two things: (a) Scripture is the one divine *source* from which, as from a spring or fountain, we draw all our theology; and (b) Scripture is the *only* norm to judge teachers and teachings in the church.

2. The Confessions, on the other hand, are the "basis, rule, and norm, indicating how all doctrines should be judged in conformity with the Word of God" (ibid., Heading). This means, quite simply, that the Confessions state what we Lutherans believe to be the teachings of Scripture and what we therefore believe, teach, and publicly confess.

3. Other good Christian writings, that is, "good, useful, and pure books, such as interpretations of the Holy Scriptures, refutations of errors, and expositions of doctrinal articles" have their place too. They are not to be rejected or spurned. "*If* they are in accord with the aforementioned pattern of doctrine [namely, the Confessions], they are to be accepted and used as helpful expositions and explanations" (ibid., 10).

Scripture, the Confessions, other good Christian literature! Scripture's authority is divine and absolute. The Confessions' authority is derived from their agreement with Scripture and is binding for everyone who professes to be a Lutheran. Other Christian writings are authoritative and useful too when they agree with Scripture and the Lutheran Confessions.

## The Confessions and Scriptural Inerrancy

Do our Lutheran Confessions teach that the Scriptures are inerrant? And do they interpret the Scriptures in such a light? There has been much debate on this issue lately, and therefore we must give the question our attention.

When we call Scripture inerrant we are using a relatively modern word to express the utter reliability and truthfulness of Scripture and of all its assertions. The term we use may be somewhat modern, but the conviction it expresses is as old as Scripture itself. The Scriptures teach and assume everywhere their utter truthfulness, and so do our Lutheran Confessions.

When our Confessions take for granted the divine origin of Scripture, they likewise take for granted its reliability and inerrancy. In our Confessions the Bible is called "the Holy Scripture of God" (FC SD, V, 3), "the clear Scripture of the Holy Spirit" (Ap, Preface, 9). Again and again "God's Word" and "Holy Scripture" are used interchangeably in our Confessions. This assurance concerning the divine origin and nature of Scripture is fundamental to a proper reading and approach to Scripture. The Lutheran Confessions consistently read Scripture as God's Word, carrying with it God's authority, God's power, God's truthfulness.

In other words, the inerrancy, or truthfulness, of Scripture is a definite result of its divine origin. And so our Lutheran Confessions speak of Scripture as "the eternal truth" (FC SD, Rule and Norm, 13). They urge us to believe the Scriptures, for "they will not lie to you" (LC, V, 76; cf. IV, 57) and cannot be "false or deceitful" (FC SD, VII, 96). And why? Because God, who is eternal Truth, cannot contradict Himself in Scripture (FC SD, XI, 35). It is His "pure, infallible, and unalterable Word" (Preface to the *Book of Concord*, p. 8).

This childlike trust in the truthfulness of Scripture permeates our Confessions as they confidently go about the business of citing and interpreting and applying the Scriptures to the great issues of their day. The power of our Confessions rests in great measure on their joyful and total submission to the divine Word.

# III. The Lutheran Confessions and the Gospel

The Lutheran Confessions were not written in a vacuum or out of any party spirit. The Lutheran Reformation was not a "revolt," as Roman Catholic historians used to call it, much less a heresy. What motivated the Reformation and the Confessions, which were its most significant fruits and its permanent legacy to us who wish to be called Lutherans today? What was the central backdrop for our Confessions, the context for these different documents which were finally incorporated in the *Book of Concord*? A reading of our Confessions will reveal that they all sprang from an urgent need to give articulation to the Gospel of Jesus Christ and to teach and give witness to this Gospel. And what is this Gospel which incited the most blessed and significant spiritual awakening since the days of the apostles?

In our Confessions (FC SD, V, 20) we read:

> The Gospel, however, is that doctrine which teaches what a man should believe in order to obtain the forgiveness of sins from God, since man has failed to keep the law of God and has transgressed it, his corrupted nature, thoughts, words, and deeds war against the law, and he is therefore subject to the wrath of God, to death, to temporal miseries, and to the punishment of hell-fire. The content of the Gospel is this, that the Son of God, Christ our Lord, himself assumed and bore the curse of the law and expiated and paid for all our sins, that through him alone we re-enter the good graces of God, obtain forgiveness of sins through faith, are freed from death and all the punishments of sin, and are saved eternally.

This statement may well be considered one of the most important and formative statements in our Lutheran Confessions. Why? Because it is the most complete and beautiful definition of the Gospel to be found in them. And that is what our Confessions are all about—the Gospel! Our great

Lutheran Confessions were written for the sake of the Gospel. The Augsburg Confession, Luther's catechisms, the Formula of Concord were not written just to blast or correct abuses in the Roman Church, or to defend Lutheran theology against the attacks of papists, or to perpetuate party spirit. These Confessions were all prompted by a faith in the Gospel, a love for it, and a determination to teach and confess it according to the Scriptures.

In this respect our Confessions resemble the New Testament itself. Paul and the other apostles preach, admonish, and say everything for the sake of the Gospel (1 Cor. 2:2; 9:16; John 20:31; 1 Peter 5:12; 1 John 5:13). That was their commission from Christ (Matt. 28:18-20; Mark 16:15).

It is remarkable how consistently our Confessions emphasize this central theme of the Gospel, how all their discussions support and lead to this theme of salvation by free grace through faith in Christ. Melanchthon in the Augsburg Confession clusters all the articles of faith around the redemptive work of Christ and justification through faith in Him. When the writers of our Formula of Concord at a later date try to settle certain controversies over original sin, the spiritual powers of man's will before conversion, the third use of the Law (as a pattern to regulate our lives), or even church usages, they make it crystal clear that their concern for the right doctrine on these matters is to enhance the Gospel and its comfort to poor sinners. When Melanchthon speaks out so strongly and at such length against the legalism and work-righteousness of the Roman Church of his day, it is only because "the Gospel (that is, the promise that sins are forgiven freely for Christ's sake) must be retained in the church" (Ap, IV, 120). And when he insists so vehemently that a sinner is justified by faith in Christ, it is because to deny or undermine this great fact "completely destroys the Gospel" (ibid.).

Martin Luther in the Smalcald Articles structures all of Christian doctrine around the simple doctrine of the Gospel, the doctrine of Christ and faith in Him. Here is what he says (SA, II, i):

> The first and chief article is this, that Jesus Christ, our God and Lord, "was put to death for our trespasses and raised again for our justification" (Rom. 4:25). He alone is "the Lamb of God, who takes away the sin of the world" (John 1:29). . . .
> Inasmuch as this must be believed and cannot be obtained or apprehended by any work, law, or merit, it is clear and

certain that such faith alone justifies us, as St. Paul says in Romans 3, "For we hold that a man is justified by faith apart from works of law" (Rom. 3:28), and again, "that he [God] himself is righteous and that he justifies him who has faith in Jesus" (Rom. 3:26).

Nothing in this article can be given up or compromised, even if heaven and earth and things temporal should be destroyed. . . .

On this article rests all that we teach and practice against the pope, the devil, and the world. Therefore we must be quite certain and have no doubts about it. . . .

This is the spirit of Luther and the Lutheran Confessions. This is why our Confessions, like Scripture itself, are always contemporary and useful. If we share this Gospel spirit, we will see how helpful and exciting our Confessions are and we will read them with avidity and profit.

# IV. The Holy Gospel and the Holy Scriptures

Now that we have defined the authority of Scripture and the meaning of the Gospel as our Confessions use these terms, we must address ourselves to the relationship between the Scriptures and the Gospel.

There is much discussion today in Lutheran circles about the relationship between Scripture and the Gospel. Certainly there is a relationship! The Gospel we preach and teach and confess is set forth in the Scriptures and normed by them. At the same time, the Scriptures, inspired by God, were written for the sake of the Gospel.

However, the idea seems to be current among some Lutheran theologians (perhaps because they have lost confidence in the inerrancy and absolute authority of Scripture) that Scripture is not the norm for Christian doctrine and therefore also for the doctrine of the Gospel. Rather the Gospel which, according to our Lutheran Confessions, is "the delightful proclamation of God's grace and favor acquired through the merits of Christ" (FC Ep, V, 7) is such a norm. This is a dangerous idea, not only because it is wrong and utterly confusing, but because it sounds so pious. The Gospel is the norm, the saying goes. There is an attractive, though deceptive, evangelical ring to that statement.

For instance, one Lutheran scholar today tells us that according to the Lutheran Confessions the Scriptures are authoritative not because of their divine origin but because of their power to judge and pardon. And another theologian says that the authority of Scripture is the power conferred upon it by God to save and to judge. The implication in both cases is that the authority of Scripture is nothing but the power of the Gospel it proclaims.

Now such a position utterly confuses the function of the Gospel with one of the functions of Scripture. It confuses the *power* of the Gospel with the *authority* of Scripture. And thus it undermines both.

Scripture is the authority for the Gospel according to our Lutheran Confessions. When Melanchthon debates with the Roman Catholics on the nature and content and function of the Gospel of justification by faith in his Apology of the Augsburg Confession (IV), his authority is always Scripture. And Scripture is authoritative, according to our Confessions, not because it contains and proclaims the Gospel—the Gospel is proclaimed in many writings—but because it is God's Word (Ap, IV, 108; XV, 14; LC, I, 121; FC SD, Rule and Norm, 10). Although our Confessions use the term "Word of God" in a number of senses, there is no doubt that they again and again identify the Scriptures with the Word of God. And that is why the Scriptures are authoritative for the teaching and preaching of the Gospel.

But if Scripture is not authoritative *because* the Gospel is contained therein, it most certainly is authoritative *for the sake of the Gospel*. In other words, the Scriptures were written for the sake of the Gospel (John 20:31; 2 Tim. 3:15). And so were our Lutheran Confessions. The authority of Scripture is not an end in itself. Our great Lutheran Confessions do not just assert their confidence in the divine authority of Scripture and then leave it at that. Their concern is always that the church under the Scriptures might propagate the Gospel Word "that alone brings salvation" (Preface to the *Book of Concord,* p. 13).   And so it is the function of Scripture to be the divine authority for evangelical teachers and teachings in the church. And it is the function of the Gospel to be the power for such teachers and teachings.

It is significant that the New Testament never calls the Gospel an authority or a norm—nor do our Lutheran Confessions. Rather it calls the Gospel power, spiritual power, power to save us forever (Rom. 1:16; 15:16; 1 Cor. 2:1-5; Eph. 1:13; 1 Thess. 2:13; 2 Tim. 1:10). And so do our Confessions.

According to our Confessions it is the Gospel that creates faith in someone's heart, brings him the Holy Spirit, and comforts him with the treasure of salvation (SA, III, iv; AC, V, 2; Ap, IV, 73; LC, II, 38). It is the Gospel that offers and confers consolation and continual forgiveness (SA, III, iii, 8). It is the Gospel by which the church lives and flourishes (Ap, VII, 20; Tr, 25; LC, II, 43, 56). It is the Gospel that incites true piety which is pleasing to God (Ap, IV, 122 ff.). And it is for the sake of the Gospel that God's fallen creation still exists (LC, II, 61 ff.).

The infallible authority of Scripture does not diminish the wonderful and saving power of the Gospel, but supports it. And the power of the Gospel does not vitiate the divine authority of Scripture. Let us leave the Gospel its power—not only when we may read it in Scripture, but wherever it is preached and taught in the church. And let us leave Scripture its authority. Then we will not only be talking sense, but we will be talking like confessional Lutherans.

# v. Who Is God?

Who is God? This is the most searching and momentous question that can occupy anyone's mind. Not the question: What is God? God is not a thing; the end of a logical syllogism; the First Cause of the deists, which does not act and cannot even be prayed to. God is not something for the philosopher to speculate about and probe, but never to find answers, like the poor surveyer in Franz Kafka's novel *The Castle*. God, as He really is, is the living, acting, saving Lord who has made Himself known in history since the creation and fall of man, who has revealed Himself in the Scriptures, revealed Himself as a righteous Judge but also as a loving Father who does not spare His own Son to save us and who gives us His Holy Spirit to bring us to a living faith in Him. That is who God is!

The person who asks: What is God?—if modern unregenerate man any longer bothers with such questions—will never find an answer. If he persists in his search, he will only wind up with an image, a caricature, or in utter frustration and nihilism.

Our Confessions know who God is. He is the God who has spoken both Law and promises to man. Everywhere the Confessions talk about God—they are *theo*centric, God-centered. But the main concern of the confessors as they write articles about God (e. g., in the Augsburg Confession, the Smalcald Articles, and the catechisms) is to give witness to the doctrine of the Trinity.

With their discussions of this subject our Confessions do not attempt to define God. No one can do that! No one has ever been able to give a definition of God. He dwells in a light which no man can approach unto (1 Tim. 6:16). One cannot limit or comprehend His majesty and essence by thought or language. We can, however, talk about Him, for He has talked about Himself in His Word, the sacred Scriptures. The Scriptures are filled with God, with descriptions of His nature and mighty works. All of Scripture is theological, language about God. And so are our Lutheran Confessions.

As expositions of Scripture they tell us who God is and what He has done for us to make us happy on earth and blessed in heaven. Like the Scriptures they do not try to exhaust the subject of God, but on the basis of Scripture they offer us a sort of piecemeal picture of our gracious God and tell us what it is necessary to know about Him to be saved.

In the three ecumenical creeds, which are included in our Lutheran Confessions, God is in each case described according to His triune nature. The Apostles' Creed describes primarily the works which are ascribed to the Father, Son, and Holy Spirit. So does the Nicene Creed, except that it emphasizes the deity of Christ the Son against various heresies of the fourth and fifth centuries.

The Athanasian Creed, which was originally a liturgical creed, written in the sixth century, goes much more deeply into the relationship between the Father and the Son and the Spirit. Each is a Person, a distinct center of consciousness, each Person uncreated, unlimited, eternal, almighty God and Lord. Yet the three Persons are one God and one Lord. And herein lies the mystery of the Trinity: one God to be worshipped in three Persons. The creed describes the relation of the Persons to each other with the following three pithy statements: "The Father was neither made nor created nor begotten by anybody. The Son was not made or created, but was begotten by the Father. The Holy Spirit was not made or created or begotten, but proceeds from the Father and the Son."

Nowhere do the Scriptures express the doctrine of the Trinity *explicitly*. But throughout the Scriptures the unity of God is taught. And also the Scriptures affirm throughout that the Father, the Son, and the Spirit are distinct, divine Persons. The ancient creeds and confessions, therefore, are drawing an obvious conclusion from the Scriptures as they articulate the doctrine of the Trinity. And every Christian is grateful as he confesses these creeds, grateful that in such a clear and beautiful way the mystery of the Godhead has been expressed in the church.

Of course, to know God means not merely that we know who He is, but what He has done. In fact, we know God primarily by what He has done for us—created us, sustained us, redeemed us through His Son, and sanctified and kept us through His Spirit. Actually, to recognize and confess God as triune, as we do in our creeds, reminds us of all He has done for us and serves to comfort and sustain us in our faith.

# VI. The Marvels of God's Creation

When our Lutheran Confessions speak of God's creation, or of redemption, or of our justification before God through faith in Christ, they are not expressing merely a hallowed doctrine of the church; they are attempting to describe and apply something that has happened, something that God has done *for us,* something that is of ultimate concern to every human being.

This is particularly apparent as we observe what our Confessions say about God's creation of all things and about His wonderful providence. The chief concern of our Lutheran Confessions as they speak of creation is not to answer questions about its time and manner. Our Confessions *assume* that God created all things out of nothing and that all things were created through His Word. And although they do not emphasize how God created the world and all things in six days, they no doubt agree with all that Luther said about this. Their chief concern is rather to *use* the fact of creation in a practical way to glorify God and to comfort us who are His creatures.

Actually there is very little said about the first creation of all things in our Confessions, except the assertion that God has made all things, as stated in our creeds. But then there is comparatively little said in Scripture about the first creation either. What our Confessions stress is that God's creation of all things was good and for man's sake. Man is the creation of a good and beneficent God, and all creation was made to serve man and does indeed serve him every moment of his life.

You may recall what Luther says in the explanation of our Small Catechism under the First Article, about creation. Not one word about those dramatic six days in which God created all things. The entire emphasis is on the *fact* that God made *me,* that He has given *me* all I have, that He sustains and

32

protects *me,* that He cares for *me* constantly, and that I am totally dependent on Him. Listen to what Luther says in his Large Catechism (II, 13-16) on this matter:

> I hold and believe that I am a creature of God; that is, that He has given and constantly sustains my body, soul, and life, my members great and small, all the faculties of my mind, my reason and understanding, and so forth; my food and drink, clothing, means of support, wife and child, servants, house and home, etc. Besides, he makes all creation help provide the comforts and necessities of life—sun, moon, and stars in the heavens, day and night, air, fire, water, the earth and all that it brings forth, birds and fish, beasts, grain and all kinds of produce. Moreover, He gives all physical and temporal blessings—good government, peace, security. Thus we learn from this article that none of us has his life of himself, or anything else that has been mentioned here or can be mentioned, nor can he by himself preserve any of them, however small and unimportant. All this is comprehended in the word "Creator."

What a marvelous doctrine this is! I am not merely an item or statistic, the result of a blind and purposeless evolution or creative urge. The world and universe are not a vast imponderable or absurdity, a mere datum to be studied. I am God's creation, His highest creation; and all the universe serves me. Even when I fell away from Him through Adam's sin He loved me and redeemed me, and now all creation serves me and all of His chosen people. God's kingdom of power, the whole creation, is totally in the service of His kingdom of grace, His Gospel.

This is a tremendously important fact for the Christian to know and build on today in our age of scientism and materialism and secularism, when we are taught that all the problems of war, economy, ecology, population, social inequality, etc., are to be solved by human planning and ingenuity. What is all this blind confidence in human achievement and planning but a virtual denial of God's continual providence, God's creation, yes, of God's very existence? For to deny or ignore that God supports and rules this universe and everything in it is to deny God altogether! Therefore we Christians who trust in God to support us and protect us and through His Holy Spirit to save us will do well in our secular age to give heed to Luther as he says in his Large Catechism (II, 23):

> We ought daily to study this article [of God's creation and

providence] and impress it upon our minds. Everything we see, and every blessing that comes our way, should remind us of it. When we escape distress or danger, we should recognize that it is God's doing. He gives us all these things so that we may sense and see in them His fatherly heart and His boundless love toward us. Thus our hearts will be warmed and kindled with gratitude to God and a desire to use all these blessings to His glory and praise.

# VII. How Man Ruined God's Creation

### Original Sin and What It Is All About

According to Scripture and the Lutheran Confessions man is the highest and noblest creature of God. God created man in His own image with holiness and knowledge and love toward God. "So original righteousness was intended to involve not only a balanced physical constitution, but these gifts as well: a surer knowledge of God, fear of God, trust in God, or at least the inclination and power to do these things. This the Scripture shows when it says that man was created in the image of God and after his likeness (Gen. 1:27)" (Ap, II, 17-18). This is something our day with its cynicism, its despair, its deep concern with what is often called dehumanization needs to hear.

According to Scripture and the Lutheran Confessions man lost his holiness and knowledge of God. Adam and Eve, the progenitors of the entire human race, rebelled against God by an act of disobedience, fell into sin, and brought sin upon all men.

> Original sin is the complete lack or absence of the original concreated righteousness of paradise or of the image of God according to which man was originally created in truth, holiness, and righteousness, together with a disability and ineptitude as far as the things of God are concerned. . . . Original sin in human nature is not only a total lack of good in spiritual, divine things, but at the same time it replaces the lost image of God in man with a deep, wicked, abominable, bottomless, inscrutable, and inexpressible corruption of his entire nature in all its powers, especially of the highest and foremost powers of the soul in mind, heart, and will (FC SD, I, 10-11).

That is what our Confessions mean by sin (cf. Rom. 5 and 7). And this too is something that our day with its confidence

35

in human planning, human technology, and its empty, naive utopias needs to hear.

Exactly what is the nature of original sin, this natural depravity of man? Our Augsburg Confession sums it up with the pithy statement that all men "since the fall of Adam . . . are without fear of God, are without trust in God, and are concupiscent" (AC, II, 1). That summarizes our condition quite concisely. Negatively we have no fear of God, no filial fear of a son toward his heavenly Father, and no trust in Him, no trust at all. But our sinfulness includes an active, positive rebellion: We are inclined by nature toward all that is evil and contrary to God. That is what is meant by concupiscence, lust: the habitual inclination of every person toward what displeases God, opposes His will, and provokes His wrath.

And what is the result of this sin, this original sin, which is no mere weakness or deficiency? Damnation, eternal damnation! Listen again to the simple, blunt language of our Augsburg Confession: "This disease or vice of origin is truly sin, which even now damns and brings eternal death on those who are not born again through Baptism and the Holy Spirit" (AC, II, 2).

According to our Lutheran Confessions man is born dead in sin—what irony: born dead (FC SD, II, 10; cf. Eph. 2:1, 5; Col. 2:13)—corrupt, helpless, incapable of approaching God or pleasing Him in any way; not free to serve God and approach those things which are above, but bound, bound like the most abject slave to everything that opposes God, to Satan (who is as real and living as God), to his own evil inclinations and a world at enmity with God.

That is man's condition, his situation. And from this native original depravity, this blindness and corruption of nature, this "root sin," as Luther calls it (SA, III, i, 1), all sins and wickednesses, all errors and stupidity, all rebellion against God and inhumanity against man proceeds. And you and I and no person on earth can do anything about it.

Except recognize our sin. And repent of it. Not as some insignificant infraction or miscalculation or mistake, but as a total perversity which condemns us all. Isaiah (1:6) describes every man's condition when he says: "From the sole of the foot even unto the head there is no soundness in it, but wounds, and bruises, and putrifying sores; they have not been closed, neither bound up, neither mollified with ointment." And Luther rightly tells us: Repentance "does not debate what is sin and what is not sin, but lumps everything

36

together and says, 'We are wholly and altogether sinful'" (SA, III, iii, 36). So we repent not so much of what we have done, but of what we are.

But what can be done about our lost condition? God has entered the picture and done something about it. According to Scripture and the Lutheran Confessions God beheld the wretched state of fallen man and sent His Son to be our Savior. The Son of God assumed human nature and reconciled the world to God. Our Confessions speak eloquently of this. It is their central message, just as it is Scripture's.

> Our churches also teach that the Word—that is, the Son of God—took on man's nature in the womb of the blessed virgin Mary. So there are two natures, divine and human, inseparably conjoined in the unity of His person, one Christ, true God and true man, who was born of the virgin Mary, truly suffered, was crucified, dead, and buried, that He might reconcile the Father to us and be a sacrifice not only for original guilt but also for all actual sins of men. He also descended into hell, and on the third day truly rose again. Afterward He ascended into heaven to sit on the right hand of the Father, forever reign and have dominion over all creatures, and sanctify those who believe in Him by sending the Holy Spirit into their hearts to rule, comfort, and quicken them and defend them against the devil and the power of sin. The same Christ will openly come again to judge the living and the dead . . . (AC, III).

What a beautiful statement of the Gospel! And this is something that our day which seems so bent on ignoring God, shouting Him down, crowding Him out of our lives and out of the universe, defining Him out of existence, needs to hear more than anything else.

### Our Knowledge of Original Sin Is Important

Many today in the Christian church think *all* a man needs to hear and know is that he is in some sense a sinner and Christ in some sense a Savior. But the Gospel cannot be understood without the Law. God's grace will never touch the human heart or make sense without a prior knowledge of sin.

Many theologians today, perhaps out of embarrassment or simple rejection of the Biblical and Confessional doctrine of sin, argue in a very reductionistic way about sin. We need not believe in a historic Adam and Eve, they say, or in a historic Fall. We need not believe in the unity of the human race, and certainly not in the idea that Adam's sin was imputed to all

37

men and that sin is inherited, which is illogical if not downright immoral. No, such notions are outmoded myths and sagas, we are told, which Scripture employs only for its own day, or perhaps incrustations of Hebrew or Pauline thought upon the "core" teaching of the Scriptures. And so we can dispence with such notions without any damage to the Gospel. Against all this Luther clearly says: "Sin had its origin in one man, Adam, though whose disobedience all men were made sinners and became subject to death and the devil" (SA, III, i, 1).

If Lutherans are suggesting such a watered down, naive reductionism today—and they are—they surely have not understood our Confessions. The Formula of Concord states: "Since the Fall man inherits an inborn wicked stamp, an interior uncleanness of the heart and evil desires and inclinations. By nature every one of us inherits from Adam a heart, sensation, and mind-set which, in its highest powers and the light of reason, is by nature diametrically opposed to God and his highest commands and is actually enmity against God, especially in divine and spiritual matters" (FC SD, I, 11; cf. also AC, II). That ought to be clear enough. And it's not a pretty picture!

Those who are too sophisticated or learned to accept the plain, unvarnished picture of sin presented in Scripture and our Confessions will not thereby enhance the Gospel; they will undermine it. The Gospel must be preached to sinners, real sinners, sinners from conception and birth, lost sinners without Christ, sinners whose sin has as real and historical an origin as their redemption in Christ. Then the Gospel enters in and "teaches what a man who has not kept the law and is condemned by it should believe, namely, that Christ has satisfied and paid for all guilt and without man's merit has obtained and won for him forgiveness of sins, the 'righteousness that avails before God,' and eternal life" (FC Ep, V, 5).

I suppose if an unbeliever were to read this chapter he would find it all terribly hard to accept. With all the cruelty and stupidity and corruption in the world, man must possess some redeeming quality. Perhaps the best answer I could offer such a person is what Luther states in the Smalcald Articles (III, i, 3): "This hereditary sin is so deep a corruption of nature that reason cannot understand it. It must be believed because of the revelation in the Scriptures (Ps. 51:5, Rom. 5:12ff., Exod. 33:20, Gen. 3:6ff.)." And there the matter stands. But I would want to tell every unbeliever about God's remedy for his spiritual depravity and his slavery to sin. And that's what the rest of this book about our Confessions is all about.

# VIII. Who Is Jesus Christ and What Has He Done?

If one were to read through our Lutheran Confessions superficially or just page through a list of the articles of faith discussed therein, one might make some rather negative judgments about them. For instance, there appears to be no sustained discussion on the saving work of Jesus Christ or the sanctifying work of the Holy Spirit or the return of Christ and eternal life. One might conclude that these fundamental emphases of the Gospel are neglected in our Confessions.

But such a conclusion would be dead wrong. In fact, these three themes, the work of Christ, the work of the Holy Spirit, and the hope of Christ's return and eternal life, pervade our Confessions and are dominant throughout. It is just this fact that gives our Confessions their evangelical character and power.

Whether our Confessions speak of original sin (FC, I) or Baptism (LC, IV) or justification (Ap, IV; FC, III) or the Lord's Supper (LC, V) or predestination (FC, XI), it is always Christ and His work that crowds into the discussion.

This is particularly true in Melanchthon's discussion of justification by faith in the fourth article of the Apology of the Augsburg Confession. This article represents the longest discussion in our Confessions and is directed against the Roman Catholic denial of justification through faith alone. It is a very controversial article. But it is only that Christ and His benefits might be known to every Christian, that Christ might be the one object of the believer's faith, that Christ might be set against the wrath of God, that His ransom and propitiation and glory might never be obscured, that Melanchthon marshalls all his arguments and expends such labor to show from the Scriptures that a sinner is justified alone by faith in Christ.

To Melanchthon, as to the apostle Paul, Christ was the

content and center of every Christian's faith and the power for every Christian's love. Christ is all this *because of what He has done for us.*

But before we speak of what Christ has done we must speak of who He is. For who He is validates everything He has done. We Christians boast not in a merely human or titular Savior, not a mere symbol for achieving meaning or fulfillment or "authentic existence" in this world, but a real Savior whose life of obedience to God and whose death as our substitute *counts* before God. And it counts because of who He is as well as what He has done.

Most readers of this little volume will recall the winsome words of Luther's Small Catechism which tell us who Jesus is: "true God, begotten of the Father from eternity, and also true man, born of the virgin Mary" (SC, II, 4). But our Confessions say much more than this about the Person of Christ. And they must do so. For in all of church history no article of the faith has been so misrepresented and mis-understood, also within the Christian church, as the article concerning the Person of Christ.

It would be far too ponderous to rehearse all the Christological heresies which have insinuated themselves upon Christ's church since the time of the apostles. Many of them have been repeated time and time again throughout the centuries of church history. The *Book of Concord* describes most of these heresies for the more inquisitive reader. I wish merely to rehearse for the reader in broad outline what our Formula of Concord says about who Christ is. Then when we understand adequately who He is, we can appreciate more fully all He has done to be our Redeemer and Savior.

### Who Then Is Jesus Christ?

Christ is God incarnate, God become man—that is who He is. He therefore possesses two natures, the divine and the human. Each nature retains its identity into all eternity, and each retains all its distinctive properties (FC SD, VIII, 6 ff.). Still, He is only one Person. Prior to the Incarnation He was only the Person of the Son of God; but now He is the Person of the God-man. Although each nature retains its identity and its attributes, the two natures are never divided or confused. As Christ lives on earth, preaches authoritatively, performs miracles and wonders, suffers, dies, and rises again, both natures work in perfect union, each doing what is proper to it. More than all this, the properties of the Godhead are actually

41

communicated permanently to the human nature, so that the human nature of Christ is all-powerful, everywhere present, omniscient. Yet the human nature retains all its own characteristics without change (FC SD, VIII, 46-64). During His humiliation on earth the human nature of Christ did not ordinarily display such divinely communicated attributes, but concealed them; but nevertheless, "In Him dwelleth all the fulness of the Godhead bodily" (Col. 2:9; cf. FC SD, VIII, 64-74).

Does all this seemingly complicated Christology which I have in only the briefest way summed up from our Formula of Concord leave us a little bewildered? Let me reply that there is purpose in such weighty discussion which occupied hundreds of volumes and millions of words at the time of the Reformation.

But first let us readily admit that there is a paradox here, a mystery which confounds the human mind—like a "square circle"—which defies analogy or even human comprehension. Think of the child Jesus in the manger: helpless, crying, nursing at His mother's breasts, dependent upon divine intervention to avoid Herod's wrath and the slaughter of the innocents! That very child is almighty God, omniscient, present everywhere, eternal, and holy. As Luther puts it in his inimitable hymn:

> He whom the world cannot enclose
> In Mary's bosom doth repose;
> To be a little child He deigns
> Who all things by Himself sustains.
>     Hallelujah!

Yes, Hallelujah! What other response is there to the mystery of the Incarnation? Who can understand it? We can only worship the Christ Child, knowing that "in Him dwelleth all the fulness of the Godhead bodily" (Col. 2:9). And as Francis Pieper, our great Lutheran dogmatician, used to say: "When we accept the Incarnation, all the other facets of our Christology which seem so difficult to ponder just fall into place, and the 'one Lord Jesus Christ' emerges, our Savior and Lord."

The Incarnation is not a mere reality, a mystery which perplexes us and then leaves us in confusion. It is a reality, a divine action, with a purpose. Our Lord, the Son of God, assumed human nature in order to save us. As one of the old

42

church fathers aptly said: "What Christ did not assume He did not redeem." Our Nicene Creed clearly states that Christ *"for us men and for our salvation* came down from heaven, was incarnate by the Holy Ghost of the Virgin Mary, and was made man." And why? That He might be "crucified under Pontius Pilate" and "suffer," suffer God's wrath against sin, *"for us."* For us! In our place! As our Substitute! Every Christian child knows this. God became a man, our Brother, our Substitute, to save us (John 3:16). That is the purpose of the Incarnation. And that is why you and I and every believer in Christ celebrate it and worship Him, the God-man.

### Christ Our Redeemer

When our Confessions speak of what Christ has done for us, they use many Biblical themes: salvation (rescue), redemption, reconciliation, propitiation, atonement, and others.

I suppose just about every reader will recall what Luther says in the explanation to the Second Article of our Small Catechism about Christ's work of redemption. There is no need to repeat this classic statement here. Actually, rather little time is given to the theme of redemption in our Confessions. Therefore let me merely offer a similar passage from Luther's Large Catechism (II, 30-31) which says much the same thing in an equally comforting way:

> Those tryrants and jailers [the devil, sin, death, God's wrath] now have been routed, and their place has been taken by Jesus Christ, the Lord of life and righteousness and every good and blessing. He has snatched us, poor lost creatures, from the jaws of hell, won us, made us free, and restored us to the Father's favor and grace. He has taken us as his own, under his protection, in order that he may rule us by his righteousness, wisdom, power, life, and blessedness.
>
> Let this be the summary of this article, that the little word "Lord" simply means the same as Redeemer, that is, he who has brought us back from the devil to God, from death to life, from sin to righteousness, and now keeps us safe there. The remaining parts of this article simply serve to clarify and express how and by what means this redemption was accomplished—that is, how much it cost Christ and what he paid and risked in order to win us and bring us under his dominion. That is to say, he became man, conceived and born without sin, of the Holy Spirit and the Virgin, that he might become Lord over sin; moreover, he suffered died, and was buried that he might make satisfaction for me and pay what I

owed, not with silver and gold but with his own precious blood. All this in order to become my Lord. For he did none of these things for himself, nor had he any need of them. Afterward he rose again from the dead, swallowed up and devoured death, and finally ascended into heaven and assumed dominion at the right hand of the Father. The devil and all powers, therefore, must be subject to him and lie beneath his feet until finally, at the last day, he will completely divide and separate us from the wicked world, the devil, death, sin, etc.

That is what Christ has done for us!

### Christ Our Reconciler

Much more is said in our Symbols about Christ's reconciliation (satisfaction), and this term seems to include all the great themes Scripture uses to describe all Christ did to save us.

We hear a great deal about "reconciliation" and "healing" in our day of conflict, revolution, alienation, and polarization in society and in the church. Such talk of reconciliation and healing is usually confined to the horizontal reconciliation between people.

Scripture and our Lutheran Confessions speak of another kind of reconciliation, that which takes place between God and man, or rather, that which has taken place once and for all through the atoning work of Jesus Christ. "God was in Christ, reconciling the world unto Himself, not imputing their trespasses unto them," Paul says (2 Cor. 5:19). And Melanchthon echoes that apostolic declaration when he says in the Augsburg Confession (III, 2-3) that Christ "was born of the virgin Mary, truly suffered, was crucified, dead, and buried, *that He might reconcile the Father to us* and be a sacrifice not only for original guilt but also for all actual sins of men."

To reconcile means to reestablish a harmonious relationship which once existed between two parties. God and man were once at peace. Adam was created in God's image and feared and loved Him. But man rebelled against God and fell into sin and spiritual death. So God took the initiative to overcome this separation and estrangement. He sent His own Son to reconcile us with Him, to satisfy His wrath against sin and all sinners, and to make peace between Himself and men.

That was the only way to do it. There was no other way.

Our Confessions say: "Men cannot keep the law by their own strength, and they are all under sin and subject to eternal wrath and death. On this account the law cannot free us from sin or justify us, but the promise of the forgiveness of sins and justification was given *because of Christ*. He was given us to make satisfaction for the sins of the world and has been appointed as the mediator and the propitiator" (Ap, IV, 40). What a tremendous comfort this is to poor sinners! Melanchthon sums it all up when he later says: "Christ is set forth to be the propitiator, through whom the Father is reconciled to us" (Ap, IV, 80).

God is reconciled, Melanchthon says, God is propitiated. And the basis of it all is Christ's work of atonement. "Christ became a sacrificial victim or trespass offering to reconcile God by his merits instead of ours. Let this stand in this issue, then, that the death of Christ is the only real propitiatory sacrifice" (Ap, XXIV, 23).

Yes, the issue is clear. But the world goes on ignoring all this, sinning, refusing to be reconciled by the death of Christ and trying rather to curry God's favor by something else than Christ's atoning work, thus rebelling against God or ignoring Him altogether.

So God appointed a ministry of reconciliation to get the all-important Word out, to tell all people what God has done and how they might share in all this, how they can be reconciled with Him (LC, II, 38).

How does this happen and how do we partake of God's reconciliation? By faith, Paul says. And our Confessions echo this great truth: "Scripture teaches that the righteousness of faith before God consists solely in a gracious reconciliation or the forgiveness of sins, which is bestowed upon us by pure grace because of the unique merit of Christ, the mediator, and which we receive only by faith in the promise of the Gospel" (FC SD, III, 30). And again our Confessions say: "Therefore, when a man believes that his sins are forgiven *because of Christ* and that *God is reconciled* and favorably disposed to him *because of Christ*, this personal faith obtains the forgiveness of sins and justifies us" (Ap, IV, 45, cf. 81).

### Christ Our Mediator

In addition to the titles "Redeemer" and "Reconciler," our Confessions very often ascribe two other titles to Christ: "Mediator" and "Propitiator." In his great Apology of the

45

Augsburg Confession Melanchthon sums up all that Christ has done for us under these two titles. Again and again he calls Christ our Propitiator and Mediator. A propitiator is one who turns away another's wrath. A mediator is one who intervenes for the guilty and pleads his case. God was angry because of our sins. And we had neither the strength nor the will to propitiate Him or mediate on our own behalf. Melanchthon portrays our situation quite correctly when he says simply: "Men cannot keep the law by their own strength, and they are all under sin and subject to eternal wrath and death" (Ap, IV, 40). So God took the initiative and gave us His Son. "He was given for us," Melanchthon says, "to make satisfaction for the sins of the world and has been appointed as the mediator and the propitiator" (ibid.). And with those mighty words Melanchthon sums up the Scriptures and the Gospel. And he gives us instructions on how we are to *use* Christ as our mediator and propitiator. How do we do this? By faith. "Faith sets against God's wrath not our merits of love, but Christ the mediator and propitiator" (Ap, IV, 46).

This is the blueprint for our happy and successful Christian life of faith. For "only faith takes hold of Christ, the propitiator" (Ap, IV, 231). "It is only by faith that Christ is accepted as the mediator. By faith alone, therefore, we obtain the forgiveness of sins when we comfort our hearts with trust in the mercy promised for Christ's sake. Paul says in Rom. 5:2, 'Through him we have obtained access' to the Father, and he adds, 'through fatih.' In this way we are reconciled to the Father and receive the forgiveness of sins when we are comforted by trust in the mercy promised for Christ's sake" (Ap, 80-81).

I suppose many might respond that such theological jargon of Melanchthon's hardly speaks to our day with all its pressing needs in terms of ecology, justice, peace, humanization (whatever that means). But Melanchthon's jargon happens to be the truth, the truth of the eternal Gospel, the "foolish" Gospel, which tells us how we can become right with God, the Gospel which has claimed us and changed us and given us new life, eternal life.

If people don't want this Gospel today, if they prefer a Christ who is a revolutionary or a social activist or perhaps just an example for something or other, then strong titles like "mediator" and "propitiator" will not speak to them.

But we who know the Christ of Scripture and our Confessions take our stand with Melanchthon and without shame say with him: "We for our part preach the foolishness of the Gospel, which reveals another righteousness, namely, that because of Christ, the propitiator, we are accounted righteous when we believe that for Christ's sake God is gracious to us" (Ap, IV, 230). That is our faith and our agenda for 1977 and as long as the world stands.

# IX. The Center of It All: Justification by Faith

*The Lutheran Confessions Focus on the Sinner's Justification Before God*

The Gospel of justification by faith, voiced so powerfully and comfortingly by the apostle Paul, was the great discovery and contribution of Martin Luther and the Reformation. Not since the days of the apostles had this Gospel message been proclaimed with such clarity and beauty. It is this central message of justification by faith, central to the Gospel and all Christian theology, which dominates our Lutheran Confessions. And it is around this doctrine that all articles and discussions in our Confessions center.

What does it means to be justified? Justification is not just an article of faith to be believed and nothing more than that. It is an event that happens to every lost sinner who comes to faith in Jesus Christ.

Commenting on Rom. 5:1, Melanchthon in the Apology of the Augsburg Confession gives the following definition of justification: "In this passage 'justify' is used in a judicial way to mean 'to absolve a guilty man and pronounce him righteous,' and to do so on account of someone else's righteousness, namely, Christ's, which is communicated to us through faith" (Ap, IV, 305).

This is a precious definition. God, the righteous Judge, absolves us, acquits us, forgives us all our sins. He does this not because we are innocent; rather He justifies us and counts us to be righteous for Christ's sake, because of His righteousness, His obedience to God's law, and His innocent suffering and death. When God justifies me He not only forgives me all my sins for Christ's sake, but He also reckons to me Christ's perfect righteousness. "Christ remains the mediator," Melanchthon says. "We must always be sure that for his sake we have a gracious God in spite of our unworthiness" (Ap, IV, 163). And our Formula of Concord (SD, III, 9) elaborates this explanation:

> We believe, teach, and confess unanimously, in accord with the summary formulation of our Christian faith and confession described above, that a poor sinner is justified before God (that is, he is absolved and declared utterly free from all his sins, and from the verdict of well deserved damnation, and is adopted as a child of God and an heir of eternal life) without any merit or worthiness on our part, and without any preceding, present, or subsequent works, by sheer grace, solely through the merit of the total obedience, the bitter passion, the death, and the resurrection of Christ, our Lord, whose obedience is reckoned to us as righteousness.

There are many things we could note from this statement which so remarkably sums up Paul's teaching on our justification before God. Here our Lutheran Church confesses (1) that Christ and His work of redemption is the basis for our justification, (2) that God justifies us freely by grace, and (3) that we receive God's justification and all its blessings through faith in Christ alone.

Our justification before God is no myth, no mere metaphor or figure of speech, no mere Pauline attempt to describe some spiritual reality or experience, but a fact, the great fact of life for us who believe in Christ. What Paul says about this fact is a literal and inspired apostolic account of how my salvation takes place.

No wonder Luther exclaimed that the discovery of this fact opened up the entire Scripture to him. No wonder Melanchthon said the doctrine of justification by faith is "the main doctrine of Christianity" because "it illumines and magnifies the honor of Christ and brings to pious consciences the abundant consolation that they need" (Ap, IV, 2). No wonder the original subscribers of the Lutheran Confessions staked their salvation on the truth of their confession which centered in the doctrine of justification. For their salvation was centered in the doctrine of justification. And so is ours!

### Justification by Faith Alone

In one of the shortest articles in the Augsburg Confession Melanchthon speaks of the most crucial issue of the entire Reformation, justification by faith. He says (AC, IV):

> Our churches also teach that men cannot be justified before God by their own strength, merits, or works but are freely

justified for Christ's sake through faith when they believe that they are received into favor and that their sins are forgiven on account of Christ, who by his death made satisfaction for our sins. This faith God imputes for righteousness in his sight (Rom. 3, 4).

It was a brief article. But it clearly presented the Lutheran position. And what a furor it caused! The papal theologians condemned it. And a year later Melanchthon wrote a lengthy defense of this simple evangelical position, a defense which represents one of the most Biblical, convincing expositions of justification by faith ever written. Melanchthon's discussion of justification, faith, and good works in the Apology is a veritable masterpiece.

We have already discussed what according to our Confessions, it means to be justified. What place does faith play in a sinner's justification? Faith is not our work or accomplishment which effects our justification before God. Our faith is rather that which *accepts* God's verdict of justification for Christ's sake. The Formula of Concord (SD, III, 13-14) says:

For faith does not justify because it is so good a work and so God-pleasing a virtue, but because it lays hold on and accepts the merit of Christ in the promise of the holy Gospel. This merit has to be applied to us and to be made our own through faith if we are to be justified thereby. Therefore the righteousness which by grace is reckoned to faith or to the believers is the obedience, the passion, and the resurrection of Christ when he satisfied the law for us and paid for our sin.

Faith is *receptivity*, receiving Christ and all He has done to save and justify us before God (Ap, IV, 48, 112). It is *confidence* in Christ and in God's mercy for Christ's sake (Ap, IV, 79). It is true *knowledge* of Christ, knowledge of all He has done to save us (Ap, IV, 46). "What is the knowledge of Christ except to know Christ's blessings?" (Ap, IV, 101). And finally, according to our Confessions faith is *personal*. No one else can believe for me, not the entire Christian church of all times. Only through *my* faith, my receiving Christ and His atoning work, will I stand before God justified: "Therefore, when a man believes that his sins are forgiven because of Christ and that God is reconciled and favorably disposed to him because of Christ, this *personal faith* obtains forgiveness of sins and justifies us" (Ap, IV, 45).

Melanchthon offers several reasons why justification can

only be received by faith *alone*. *First*, since everything Christ has done for us is announced to us through a promise, the Gospel, a verdict of acquittal, faith is the only possible instrument which can accept such a verdict or promise. There is no other way to receive a verdict or promise except by believing it (Ap, IV, 61-72). *Second*, sinful man, depraved and evil by nature, cannot by his own piety or good works merit justification before God. Rather, he merits the very opposite, condemnation; and he insults Christ, who came to bring him salvation full and free and make him righteous before God, by not simply believing the promises (Ap, IV, 29 ff.). *Third*, the Law cannot save us or justify us; only the Gospel can do that. The Law may maintain outward discipline in the world, but man's feeble attempt to obey it cannot satisfy God's justice (Ap, IV, 22 ff.). Furthermore, the Law functions always to accuse and frighten us (Ap, IV, 37-38, 257). *Finally*, no one can obey the Law and thus be justified by it; rather, the Gospel cancels the verdict of the Law—thank God—and tells us that we are justified by His grace for Christ's sake (Ap, IV, 157-158).

I suppose again many today would call all this discussion needless quibbling. But only because so many today do not understand the despair that comes to one who tries to approach a righteous God on his own terms. What a comfort it is, Melanchthon and Luther reiterate, to know that God is at peace with us for Christ's sake and that we need only believe in His promises and grace (Ap, IV, 85, 119, 148, 204, 285, 382)! Then we can have certainty that we have a loving and gracious God and can stand before Him, clothed in Christ's righteousness, and serve Him in love and gratitude.

# x. The Work of the Spirit

I suppose the criticisms from several sources that Lutherans today do not sufficiently emphasize the work of the Holy Spirit are well taken. How often do we really sing and pray to the Holy Spirit, proclaim His work in our pulpits, and thank God for His presence and gifts? Perhaps it is such apathy and neglect of the Spirit and His work that has led many Lutherans today to identify with Pentecostalism and other aberrant movements which stress, although often wrongly, the activity of the Spirit and His presence in and among Christians.

Such criticism, however, could never have been leveled against Luther and the other Reformers who wrote our Confessions. For not only do our Lutheran Confessions proclaim the Spirit-breathed theology of Scripture, not only do they reveal the Spirit-filled life and testimony of their authors, but they emphasize throughout in a remarkable manner the saving and comforting work of the Spirit in the life of every believer and throughout the church. One need only recall the words of Luther in his explanation to the Third Article (SC, II, 6) to appreciate the beauty and power with which Lutheranism has expressed this great and comforting fact:

> The Holy Spirit has called me through the Gospel, enlighten-ed me with his gifts, and sanctified and preserved me in true faith, just as he calls, gathers, enlightens, and sanctifies the whole Christian church on earth and preserves it in union with Jesus Christ in the one true faith. In this Christian church he daily and abundantly forgives all my sins, and the sins of all believers, and on the last day he will raise me and all the dead and will grant eternal life to me and to all who believe in Christ.

Specifically two things are mentioned repeatedly in our Confessions about the work of the Holy Spirit.

1. *First,* our Confessions emphasize the Spirit's activity

as Comforter to work faith in us through the Gospel (AC, V, 2), to "sanctify, purify, strengthen, and comfort all who believe in [Christ]" (AC, III, 4). Luther says (LC, II, 38):

> Neither you nor I could ever know anything of Christ, or believe in him and take him as our Lord, unless these were first offered to us and bestowed on our hearts through the preaching of the Gospel by the Holy Spirit. The work is finished and completed, Christ has acquired and won the treasure for us by his sufferings, death, and resurrection, etc. But if the work remained hidden and no one knew of it, it would have been all in vain, all lost. In order that this treasure might not be buried but put to use and enjoyed, God has caused the Word to be published and proclaimed, in which he has given the Holy Spirit to offer and apply to us this treasure of salvation.

2. *Second,* our Confessions emphasize that the Holy Spirit, whom we receive by faith, dwells in us and enables us to live a life for God. "Without the Holy Spirit we cannot keep the law," the Apology says (IV, 135). But when we are justified and regenerated through faith in the Gospel "we receive the Holy Spirit" (Ap, IV, 126, 133, 135), who not only comforts us (FC SD, V, 11), governs and defends us from all error (Ap, IV, 139), and makes the Gospel clear to us (Ap, IV, 230), but also helps us to mortify our sin (Ap, II, 45), resist it (Ap, IV, 146), war against the law in our members (SA, III, iii, 40), lead a pure and godly life, and persevere in the faith. Yes, the Spirit works not only faith in our hearts but love as well, the only love that will ever please God, love toward God and our fellowman (FC SD, III, 23). And the "good works" produced by such love are the testimonies that the Spirit dwells in us (FC Ep, V, 15).

And so our Confessions everywhere stress the work of the Holy Spirit, His work, His exclusive work, in converting and regenerating and justifying us, and His work, His exclusive work, in sanctifying us and keeping us God's children.

But they say rather little about the "extraordinary" gifts which are stressed by the sects today, e. g., healing, casting out demons, speaking in tongues, etc. Why? Clearly because the two great works of the Spirit, to bring Christ to us and to work the Christian life in us, are of such palmary and overarching importance! *The ministry of the Spirit is the ministry of the Gospel* (AC, V). That is the important thing. After all, the Roman church claimed miracles, healings, exorcism; but with all the emphasis on salvation by good works it buried Christ and obscured the Gospel (AP, IV, 81, 110, 121).

Today too the ministry of the Spirit is the ministry of the Gospel. And we had best shun all the fantastic claims of the sects which assert that they have an extraordinary out-pouring of the Spirit, but are not able to preach the Gospel in all its purity.

Rather let us seek the Spirit in His Gospel Word, where Christ is preached. He is after all the Third Person of the Trinity, the Comforter, sent by the Father and the Son to testify of the Son (John 15:26) and glorify Him (John 16:14). To separate His saving activity today from Christ's past saving work is heresy. The Spirit is present with all His saving gifts where Christ is preached, and He is present in our hearts. And when we have Christ we have all things.

### The Ministry of the Holy Spirit

If you could have listened to the many theological discussions and read the many textbooks on Christian doctrine during the past generations, you would have discovered a great deal of interest in the subject of church and ministry. The words were always in that order: church and ministry. The emphasis was on the church, and the church has a ministry. And the ministry was thought to be the office of pastor.

Now I don't wish to quarrel with that way of speaking. But it is interesting that our Lutheran Confessions don't usually talk that way. In the Augsburg Confession Melanchthon speaks first about the ministry (Article V) and only later about the church (Articles VII, VIII) and about pastors and preachers (Article XIV). In his Large Catechism Luther does the same as he offers his explanation of the Third Article of the Creed on the work of the Holy Spirit.

Listen to what Melanchthon says. He has just been talking of being justified by faith, and he states (AC, V):

> To obtain such faith God instituted the office of the ministry, that is, provided the Gospel and the sacraments. Through these, as through means, he gives the Holy Spirit, who works faith, when and where he pleases, in those who hear the Gospel. And the Gospel teaches that we have a gracious God, not by our own merits but by the merits of Christ, when we believe this.

Notice! Not a word about the church and not a word about

54

pastors and teachers in the church. To Melanchthon the ministry is not first of all the pastoral office (we will be speaking about pastors and ministers later) but the Spirit's office, His work of creating faith in Christ through the Gospel and the sacraments.

It is through the ministry of the Gospel Word and sacraments that the Spirit of God creates and builds His church. This church then becomes the place where the Spirit does His work of saving lost sinners. The Spirit, says Luther, "first leads us into his holy community, placing us upon the bosom of the church, where he preaches to us and brings us to Christ" (LC, II, 37).

Luther is most emphatic that the Spirit does all this Himself and does it all only through the ministry of the Gospel Word and through the sacraments. "Where Christ is not preached, there is no Holy Spirit to create, call, and gather the Christian church, and outside it no one can come to the Lord Christ" (LC, II, 45). Again we notice that Luther does not even mention preachers and teachers—so taken up is he, so enthralled, by the Spirit's activity through the Word to bring us all the benefits Christ has acquired for us by His life and death and resurrection, by His ascension and sitting at God's right hand; so captivated is he by the Spirit's activity to bring us, through that same Gospel Word, God's forgiveness, comfort, peace, and the certain hope of eternal blessedness with Him. Oh, if only we could recapture some of Luther's intense joy and (one might say) preoccupation with the Holy Spirit's work and ministry to bless us and save us! Listen as he speaks eloquently on the subject (LC, II, 61-62):

> This, then, is the article which must always remain in force. Creation is past and redemption is accomplished, but the Holy Spirit carries on his work unceasingly until the last day. For this purpose he has appointed a community on earth, through which he speaks and does all his work. For he has not yet gathered together all his Christian people, nor has he completed the granting of forgiveness. Therefore we believe in him who daily brings us into this community through the Word, and imparts, increases, and strengthens faith through the same Word and the forgiveness of sins. Then when his work has been finished and we abide in it, having died to the world and all evil, he will finally make us perfectly and eternally holy. We now wait in faith for this to be accomplished through the Word.

Our Lutheran Confessions by no means ignore or demean

pastors and preachers and their importance as instruments of the Spirit. But with their strong emphasis on the work and ministry of the Spirit, who alone converts and comforts and saves us through the Word, perhaps our Confessions say something significant for us today. Today we are told that people, Christian people and especially the young, are wary and highly critical of the institutional church and of many pastors and theologians who often seem out of touch with their real spiritual needs. If this is so, such people should be reminded that the Spirit has not abdicated His ministry, but is still active, graciously and wondrously active, in His community, the church, wherever the Word is proclaimed and the sacraments are administered. If, like our Confessions, we today can focus people's attention on the Spirit of God and His ministry, if poor sinners young and old can experience His saving and sanctifying work in their lives, then they will appreciate too the meaning of Spirit-wrought Christian fellowship and will perceive that the church, as Luther put it, is indeed "a unique community in the world" (LC, II, 42). And then too they will love and honor Christian pastors and teachers as the Spirit's ministers, as having also "the ministry of the Word," and they will "know that God approves this ministry and is present in it" (Ap, XIII, 12-13).

# XI. The Church and Its Pastors

"Thank God," Luther says, "a seven-year-old child knows what the church is, namely, holy believers and sheep who hear the voice of their Shepherd" (SA, III, xii, 2). That statement of Luther's, so blunt and pithy and typical of him, was not exactly true. He was referring to Lutheran children. The Roman Catholics of his day had the most distorted and confused ideas of what the church was: they thought it was the papacy, or the clergy, or the external ecclesiastical institution with all its ceremonies.

Luther's understanding and definition of the church represented a tremendous exegetical breakthrough, a momentous discovery. Just as his deep study of Scripture finally brought him to a knowledge of how a lost sinner is justified, that study also brought him to a knowledge of what the church really is.

Again Luther discovered wherein the real holiness of the church consisted: not in "surplices, tonsures, albs, or other ceremonies of theirs [the papists] which they have invented over and above the Holy Scriptures, but it consists of the Word of God and true faith" (ibid., 3).

Melanchthon, seven years before Luther, had defined the church in his usually more precise manner: "Our churches also teach that one holy church is to continue forever. The church is the assembly of saints in which the Gospel is taught purely and the sacraments are administered rightly" (AC, VII, 1). He adds a little to Luther's definition when he says not only who constitutes the church, namely all saints (or believers), but speaks further of the marks of the church, the signs, which indicate where it may be found. This was necessary, for if the church consists of all believers, and no one can look into another's heart and see his faith (only God can do that!), how can we know *where* the church *is*? And that was an important question in those days when Roman Catholics were saying, "We are the church," and Enthusiasts and Anabaptists and others were saying, "We are the church."

Actually Melanchthon, when he speaks of the marks of the church, is speaking of the same thing as Luther, when he spoke of what makes the church holy. The Holy Spirit makes the church holy through the external marks of the Gospel Word and the sacraments. Those signposts which tell us where the church is are the very instruments and power by which the Spirit of God creates and sustains the church in the first place.

How simple is our Lutheran doctrine of the church! No wonder Luther said any seven-year-old child knows what the church is. And no wonder Melanchthon's definition was so short.

But of course this definition did not go unchallenged in those days. Roman Catholic theologians attacked the Lutherans and insisted that the oneness, or unity, of the church depended on being under the papacy and observing the same human traditions and rites and ceremonies everywhere. They accused the Lutherans of heresy at this point. And it became necessary for Melanchthon to defend the Lutheran position at length not only in his Apology of the Augsburg Confession but six years later in his Treatise on the Power and Primacy of the Pope, in which he not only denies that the papacy with its hierarchy is the church with the power of the keys and power even to transfer secular kingdoms; but because the pope proclaims himself to be the vicar of Christ on earth and declares that it is necessary for salvation to believe what he teaches (Tr, 3), Melanchthon asserts that the papacy is the very Antichrist (Tr, 39 ff.), prophesied by the apostle Paul in 2 Thess. 2, who would arise from within the church and deceive Christians by "impious doctrines and blasphemies" and thus deny the very Gospel of salvation by grace alone.

Other sects in those days denied the Lutheran doctrine of the marks of the church too. The Enthusiasts and Anabaptists believed they could achieve a pure church without hypocrites ever associated with it, and they spurned the idea that the Spirit worked exclusively through the Scriptures and spoken Word and sacraments (SA, III, viii, 3). Against these "spiritualists" who boasted that they had the Holy Spirit Luther reacted violently: "All this is the old devil and the old serpent" (ibid., 5). Later the Calvinists added a third mark of the church, namely, external discipline in the church. This was quite contrary to the Lutheran position, for the children of the world can maintain outward discipline to some degree (Ap, IV, 4 ff.). Frankly, I believe that such an innovation by the Calvinists on this point marks the beginnings of some of the real evils of later Pietism among both Calvinists and Lutherans. For this new mark, which can be construed in so many divergent ways, tends to make Christians pharisaical or to deprive them of the full comfort of an unconditioned Gospel.

The Lutheran doctrine of the church is wonderfully comforting. It agrees perfectly with the doctrine that a sinner is saved and justified by grace alone without works, and it agrees with the doctrine that the Spirit of God alone works faith in our hearts and keeps us in Christ's church. Nothing more convincingly affirms the comfort in Luther's doctrine of the church than his classic words in the Large Catechism (II, 51-53):

> This is the sum and substance of this phrase: I believe that there is on earth a little holy flock or community of pure saints under one head, Christ. It is called together by the Holy Spirit in one faith, mind, and understanding. It possesses a variety of gifts, yet is united in love without sect or schism. Of this community I also am a part and member, a participant and co-partner in all the blessings it possesses. I was brought to it by the Holy Spirit and incorporated into it through the fact that I have heard and still hear God's Word, which is the first step in entering it. Before we had advanced this far, we were entirely of the devil, knowing nothing of God and of Christ. Until the last day the Holy Spirit remains with the holy community or Christian people. Through it he gathers us, using it to teach and preach the Word. By it he creates and increases sanctification, causing it daily to grow and become strong in the faith and in the fruits of the Spirit.

### Ministers in the Church

The mission of the church, as our Confessions testify throughout, is to preach the Gospel and administer the sacraments. Local churches everywhere do this publicly and in an orderly way by calling and ordaining pastors and teachers and ministers. "For wherever the church exists, the right to administer the Gospel also exists. Wherefore it is necessary for the church to retain the right of calling, electing, and ordaining ministers" (Tr, 67). So far as I can tell,

59

our confessions use such words as pastor (shepherd), minister (servant of the Word), teacher (doctor), presbyter (elder), bishop (overseer), or clergyman all interchangeably (cf. AC, XIV, also Tr, 61, 62, 65, 67, 72). Christ did not ordain any rank or order among the pastors and ministers and teachers with their differing gifts (Tr, 7-11), although the Lutherans retained bishops and ranks among the clergy as a human arrangement. The congregations' right to call and ordain pastors is not a mere option that the church may or may not exercise. The office of pastor is not a matter of Christian liberty. The church *must* ordain pastors, public ministers of the Word (Tr, 72). It is a "command" of God (Ap, XIII, 12).

Just how the churches call, elect, and ordain is not set forth in our Confessions. The how of it all is a matter of Christian liberty. In some cases a pastor would apply for a call, in other cases a bishop (who occupied a higher rank in the church only by human right) or a prince would arrange for the call and ordination of a pastor. Usually the congregation itself would attend to such matters. But it was *always* done. "Our churches teach that nobody should preach publicly in the church or administer the sacraments unless he is regularly called" (AC, XIV). And the call, election, and ordination always went together in those days, like the Word and water in Baptism, to establish a qualified man as pastor or teacher in the church. The Roman Catholic doctrine that ordination was a sacrament which altered the character of a minister is rejected by our Confessions, although Melanchthon has no objection to calling it a "sacrament" if it "is interpreted in relation to the ministry of the Word" (Ap, XIII, 11). The "laying on of hands" or "ordination," usually by a bishop, was "to confirm" a proper election and call (Tr, 70).

The authority or power belonging to ministers has been *given by Christ Himself* and is exactly the same authority given the apostles, although pastors today do not possess all the supernatural gifts the apostles had. The authority is only a "spiritual power" (Tr, 31). The power is essentially the public administration of the office of the keys, which is given to the entire church or community of believers (Tr, 24). Usually it is called simply "the ministry of the Word" (Ap, XIII, 11-13) or "the ministry of the Gospel" (Tr, 34; cf. SA, III, iv). The office, or work, of the pastor or minister is summed up as follows: "The Gospel [i. e., Scripture] requires of those who preside over the churches that they preach the Gospel, remit sins, administer the sacraments, and, in addition, exercise jurisdiction, that is, excommunicate those who are guilty of notorious crimes and absolve those who repent" (Tr, 60; AC, XXVIII, 5). That ought to be enough to keep any pastor busy. His mission is not to involve himself in civil government (AC, XXVIII, 2), although as a private citizen he may take an active part in the social and temporal affairs of civil government.

I think it is interesting that Melanchthon above says that it is within the province of the pastor as he publicly administers the keys to excommunicate impenitent sinners (cf. AC, XXVIII, 21). This might seem to be out of harmony with the Lutheran practice in our country, where the congregation has pretty well reserved that prerogative to itself, although no doubt in those days the pastor was always acting on behalf of the congregation and as its representative. I can find no evidence in our Confessions that congregations or synods as such carried out excommunication, and Matt. 18:15-20 is never used in our Confessions as a model for congregational discipline or excommunication, although this may have been an oversight.

Needless to say, the spiritual power of the keys conferred upon the minister publicly to preach and apply the Gospel and even to retain sins and excommunicate is a great one indeed, transcending all power in the civil domain or in nature, a truly awesome responsibility. Therefore the office of minister was held in highest reverence by the people of that day—not because of his person, but because his office was to preach the Word of God, just as his office depended on that Word (cf. Ap, XV, 41 ff.).

61

# XII. The Work of the Law and the Gospel: Repentance

Apart from the doctrine of justification by faith, no subjects dominate the discussions in our Confessions more than the topics of Law and Gospel and of repentance. Actually the two topics belong together and are often treated together in our Confessions (Ap, IV, XII; FC, V).

Why are these two themes so important to the Reformers and to our Confessions? First, because Roman Catholicism had utterly distorted the Gospel and "buried Christ" by a false doctrine of repentance, which was called the Sacrament of Penance and was completely work-righteous. But second, because of the intrinsic importance of knowing how to distinguish between Law and Gospel and of the absolute necessity of repentance. For eternal life is not offered one person who will not repent.

What is repentance? Our Augsburg Confession (XII, 3-5) answers the question concisely and in strict accordance with the Biblical teaching: "Properly speaking, repentance consists of these two parts: one is contrition, that is, terror smiting the conscience with a knowledge of sin, and the other is faith, which is born of the Gospel, or of absolution, believes that sins are forgiven for Christ's sake, comforts the conscience, and delivers it from terror." Melanchthon expends pages in his Apology (XII, 44-52) defending and explaining this definition according to Scripture; his discussion of the subject is magnificent.

I have often thought that Melanchthon's definition of repentance, which is so common to our Confessions, must seem anachronistic to even the most orthodox and dedicated Christians and Lutherans today. It is so utterly radical. How often does he speak of contrition as "mortifying" the flesh, "terrors of conscience," and the feeling of "God's wrath" against sin (Ap, IV, 142). And Luther uses even stronger words. Contrition is "drowning" the Old Adam "daily" (SC, IV, 12), despairing of any accomplishments we might render God. "One thing is sure," Luther says: "We cannot pin our hope on anything that we are, think, say, or do. And so our repentance cannot be false, uncertain, or partial, for a person who confesses that he is altogether sinful embraces all sins in his confession without omitting or forgetting a single one" (SA, III, iii, 36-37).

And the second part of repentance, faith, is just as radical as the first, contrition. We have already spoken at length about what faith is and does. Let me at this point cite just one statement from Melanchthon (Ap, IV, 345-347):

> Properly speaking, the Gospel is the command to believe that we have a gracious God because of Christ. "God sent the Son into the world, not to condemn the world, but that the world might be saved through him. He who believes in him is not condemned," etc. (John 3:17, 18). So whenever mercy is spoken of, faith in the promise must be added. This faith produces a sure hope, for it rests on the Word and commandment of God. If our hope were to rest on works, then it would really be unsure since works cannot still the conscience, as we have often said above. This faith makes the difference between those who are saved and those who are not. Faith makes the difference between the worthy and the unworthy because eternal life is promised to the justified and it is faith that justifies.

This is the sum and substance of repentance, contrition, and faith. And the Christian's life is a life of repentance.

Neither contrition nor faith is something we work out for ourselves. The Holy Spirit works both in us. He works contrition through the Law, and exclusively through the Law; and He works faith through the Gospel, and exclusively through the Gospel. The most important distinction between Law and Gospel lies in just this fact. Melanchthon puts it well: "These are the two chief works of God in men, to terrify and to justify and quicken the terrified. One or the other of these works is spoken of throughout Scripture. One part is the law, which reveals, denounces, and condemns sin. The other part is the Gospel, that is, the promise of grace granted in Christ" (Ap, XII, 53).

# XIII. Baptism

No Christian since apostolic days ever wrote more eloquently and convincingly about Holy Baptism than Luther. He was able to do so because it meant so much to him. I imagine that a day scarcely passed in his life when he did not think of his baptism and thank God for it and recall what God said to him and did for him there. His greatest regret when he knew he would die was that he would be unable to write another book on the subject.

Although the Augsburg Confession and the Apology speak about Baptism, that it is necessary for salvation, that it offers the grace of God, and that infants ought to be baptized (AC, IX; Ap, IX), it is to the two catechisms of Luther that we must repair if we are to find the doctrine taught with all its power and comfort. Here Luther shows himself to be very systematic: First, he speaks of what it is and what it bestows upon us; second, he speaks of how it can produce such great effects; and third, he speaks of how it affects our lives every day and how we are to use it.

Baptism was instituted by Christ (Matt. 28:19) Himself as a way in which "we are first received into the Christian community" (LC, IV, 2). It is not a mere washing or immersion in water, but because God's Word and command are added to it, it becomes "a divine, heavenly, holy, and blessed water" (ibid., 17). As St. Augustine said, when the Word is added to the element or substance, a sacrament takes place, a holy act which brings blessings to those who receive it.

And what are the blessings of Baptism? "To put it most simply, the power, effect, benefit, fruit, and purpose of Baptism is to save" (ibid., 24). Luther insists that Baptism is not something we do, but through Baptism God is working in us. In this sense it is "God himself" who baptizes us (ibid., 10). "Baptism is not a work which we do but is a treasure which God gives us and faith grasps, just as the Lord Christ upon the cross is not a work but a treasure comprehended and offered to us in the Word and received by faith" (ibid., 37). Luther calls it "Christ's baptism" because through Baptism everything our Savior has procured and accomplished for us becomes ours. It is truly an instrument through which the Holy Spirit and faith are given (AC, V).

Many in Luther's day thought his doctrine of Baptism was too Romish; he had not reformed the church enough at this point. A main criticism was that one ought to believe before he is baptized. Luther agreed with this and maintained that Baptism, like the Lord's Supper, must be received by faith. "Faith clings to the water and believes it to be Baptism in which there is sheer salvation and life, not through the water, as we have sufficiently stated, but through its incorporation with God's Word and ordinance and the joining of his name to it" (LC, IV, 29). Again and again our Confessions insist that the sacraments are "intended to awaken and confirm faith in those who use them" (AC, XIII, 1-2). Melanchthon says: "Thus we teach that in using the sacraments there must be a faith which believes these promises and accepts that which is promised and offered in the sacrament. The reason for this is clear and well founded. A promise is useless unless faith accepts it" (Ap, XIII, 19-20).

But what about infants? How can they have faith to accept the stupendous promises of Baptism? Luther replies that if infants can have the Holy Spirit, which is taught throughout Scripture, they can certainly have faith (LC, IV, 49 ff.). Furthermore, he says, "We bring the child with the purpose and hope that he may believe, and we pray God to grant him faith" (ibid., 57). Luther believes that Baptism, like the Gospel, is powerful to confer the very faith it calls for with its promises, and in each case the Holy Spirit monergistically (i. e., exclusively, without any cooperation from the one baptized) works faith through the instruments of His choosing, namely Baptism and the Gospel. It is no more difficult or incredible for Him to work faith in infants through the Gospel promise in Baptism than in adults through the preaching of the Gospel.

Baptism is not something that happens once and then there is no more to it. Its power and effect last throughout our lives. It initiates the life of repentance, the struggle, the never-ending struggle, of the Christian to put off his flesh, that "irascible, spiteful, envious, unchaste, greedy, lazy, proud, yes, and unbelieving" nature of ours, and to live a life of the Spirit, a life of righteousness and good works (ibid., 66-67). And Baptism, that simple act which happened so long ago in the lives of most of us, gives us the power to do just that! Amazing grace!

Luther preferred Baptism by immersion. He speaks of "being dipped into the water, which covers us completely, and being drawn out again" (ibid., 65). And he speaks of being "plunged" into Baptism. Immersion was not a necessary mode of Baptism to him, but it graphically illustrated and signified the struggle in the Christian's life of repentance. "When we become Christians, the old man daily decreases until he is finally destroyed. This is what it means to plunge into Baptism and daily come forth again" (ibid., 71). That is how we use our baptism: We "plunge" into it and its promises every day, and then emerge renewed and strengthened to live the life of faith.

# XIV. The Lord's Supper

Luther fought three great doctrinal controversies in his life. First was his struggle to maintain justification by grace for Christ's sake through faith, against Roman Catholic work-righteousness. Second was his struggle against the Enthusiasts, who claimed that the Holy Spirit did not work through means such as the Gospel Word and the sacraments, but directly. Third was his controversy with the Reformed, Ulrich Zwingli, Martin Bucer, and others from Switzerland and South Germany concerning the Lord's Supper. In the first case the very heart and comfort of the Biblical Gospel was denied by the adversaries. In the second case any objective and cognitive basis for Christian doctrine was undermined, for the Enthusiasts based their religion on their own private experiences and revelations. In the third case the Reformed believed in justification by faith, as did the Lutherans, and in the objective authority of Scripture. But they brought with them an approach to Scripture which Luther could not stand: They applied certain rationalistic principles of interpretation to the Scriptures, and when these principles were applied to Christ's words of institution of the Lord's Supper, a great controversy ensued.

At first Zwingli taught "that the Lord's Supper was only an external sign whereby one can identify Christians," and the bread and wine distributed in the Sacrament are merely "signs of the absent body of Christ" (FC SD, 4). After much controversy John Calvin, a later reformer from Geneva, modified the doctrine somewhat, saying that Christ is present in the Supper according to His divine nature (just as the divine nature is present everywhere) and "that through the Spirit of Christ, which is everywhere, our bodies, in which the Spirit of Christ dwells here upon earth, are united with the body of Christ, which is in heaven" (ibid., 4-5).

This sort of interpretation was based on the principle that the body of Christ, which was thought to be finite and therefore subject absolutely to the conditions of space and time, could not be present in more than one place at one time. Calvin could speak of a "spiritual" eating (of faith) in the Lord's Supper. But, like all the Reformed before and after him, he denied what Luther had written in his Small Catechism (VI, 2) in 1529: "[The Sacrament of the Altar], instituted by Christ himself, is the true body and blood of our Lord Jesus Christ, under the bread and wine, given to us Christians to eat and to drink."

All through his life Luther battled against every denial of the real and essential presence of Christ's body and blood in the Sacrament of the Altar, whatever form that denial took. To him Christ's words of institution recorded in the Bible were clear for any Christian to understand; and they cannot be taken in any flowery or figurative sense, but must be understood literally, as they read: "Take, eat; this is my body, which is given for you. . . . This cup is the new testament in my blood, which is poured out for you for the forgiveness of sins" (LC, V, 3, cf. 8).

The Formula of Concord summarizes Luther as the writers there present the Lutheran doctrine of the Real Presence. 1. It is the natural and usual and correct procedure to take words of command and promise literally unless there is some compelling reason for not doing so. If the words of institution were to be taken figuratively, simply because they seem to conflict with reason, or common sense, we could do so with any command or promise of God. Perhaps Abraham should then have taken God's command to sacrifice his only son just figuratively, whatever that might have meant. Such manner of interpretation would undermine all God's commands and promises, which often transcend reason and understanding (FC SD, VII, 45-47). 2. The Lord's Supper was instituted by Christ in the context of His last will and testament. On such an occasion one does not employ flowery language, but "the most appropriate, simple, in-dubitable, and clear words," as in the case of other covenant signs, like Baptism or circumcision (ibid., 48-51). 3. All three evangelists who record Christ's institution and Paul agree in their wording of the institution, and in no case is there a hint that a figurative interpretation should be given to Christ's words (ibid., 52-53). 4. Finally, Paul speaks in 1 Cor. 10:16 of a communion (togetherness), or participation, of the bread with the body of Christ and of the wine with the blood in the Sacrament. And "if the body of Christ were not truly and essentially present . . . then the bread could not be called participation in the body" (ibid., 55). Paul "says that the bread is participation in the body of Christ, and that means that all who receive the blessed bread also partake of the body of Christ. Therefore he certainly cannot be speaking of a spiritual eating but of a sacramental or oral eating of the body of Christ in which both the godly and the godless participate" (ibid., 56).

Of course, we do not eat Christ's body and blood in the same way as we munch on a hamburger and sip a Coca Cola (FC Ep, VII, 41-42). The Reformed accused Luther of such a crass doctrine. The Christ who existed in His mother's womb and yet was everywhere present, who could appear to His disciples after His resurrection through closed and locked doors, who today is at the right hand of God, which is everywhere, can be present also today among His people in various ways. He is with us when we pray in His name, not in such a way that we see or feel Him, but really and truly present, the incarnate Christ, according to both divine and human natures. And He is present with His body and blood in the Sacrament of the Altar, present with His grace, forgiveness, eternal life, and all the gifts which by His body and blood He has procured for us. All this "transcends nature and reason, even the comprehension of all the angels in heaven" (FC SD, VII, 102). But it is true, nevertheless. "The Word of God is not false or deceitful" (ibid., 96). And Luther says: "I do not want to deny in any way that God's power is able to make a body be simultaneously in many places, even in a corporeal and comprehensible manner" (ibid., 103).

Luther was adamant in his opposition to all who would deny that Christ's words of institution actually bring about the presence of Christ's body and blood in the Sacrament and that we who partake of the Supper actually, with the mouth, eat His body and drink His blood. Shortly before his death he wrote with great fervor: "I reckon them all as belonging together (that is, as Sacramentarians and enthusiasts), for that is what they are who will not believe that the Lord's bread in the Supper is his true, natural body, which the godless or Judas receive orally as well as St. Peter and all the saints. Whoever, I say, will not believe this, will please let me alone and expect no fellowship from me. This is final" (ibid., 33; cf. WA, 54, 155-156).

Why such vehemence and pugnacious stubbornness? For hundreds of years our Reformed friends and others have criticized Luther for his intransigence and refusal to compromise on the Real Presence. Why Luther's attitude?

Luther had two very good reasons. First, because he believed, and all true Lutherans with him, in the *truthfulness* of the divine Word, whether the Word instituted the Lord's Supper, or Baptism, or proclaimed the forgiveness of sins for Christ's sake. No Lutheran will tamper with the Word or try to twist it to say anything but its intended meaning. "We know that God does not lie. My neighbor and I—in short, all men—may err and deceive, but God's Word cannot err" (LC, IV, 57).

Second, Luther and Lutheran theology held so tenaciously to the Real Presence because Lutherans believed in the *power* of the divine Word. When God said at the creation, "Let there be light," there was light. When Christ instituted the sacrament of His body and blood, that is what happens, the Word creates the reality: Christ's body and blood are present for Christians to eat and drink. Luther says (FC SD, VII, 74-75):

> No man's word or work, be it the merit or the speaking of the minister, be it the eating and drinking or the faith of the communicants, can effect the true presence of the body and blood of Christ in the Supper. This is to be ascribed only to the almighty power of God and the Word, institution, and ordinance of our Lord Jesus Christ. For the truthful and *almighty words* of Jesus Christ which he spoke in the first institution were not only efficacious in the first Supper but they still retain their validity and efficacious power in all places where the Supper is observed according to Christ's institution and where his words are used, and the body and blood of Christ are truly present, distributed, and received by the virtue and potency of the same words which Christ spoke in the first Supper. For wherever we observe his institution and speak his words over the bread and cup and distribute the blessed bread and cup, Christ himself is still active through the spoken words by the virtue of the first institution, which he wants to be repeated.

But what value is there in eating and drinking Christ's body and blood? Perhaps this is just some sort of medieval, mystical interpretive incrustation which has no meaning and should have been discarded by Luther, as Zwingli and so many others did. Not at all!

Luther saw with deep penetration the true meaning of the Lord's Supper and the Real Presence. In the Supper Christ invites us to eat His actual body "which was given for you" and to drink His real blood "which was shed for you and for many." With His body and blood we receive everything that Christ by His body and blood procured for us: forgiveness, reconciliation with God, peace in our hearts, eternal life— every spiritual blessing God can give! Luther says: "Therefore it is absurd to say that Christ's body and blood are not given and poured out for us in the Lord's Supper and hence that we cannot have forgiveness of sins in the sacrament. Although the work was accomplished and forgiveness of sins was acquired on the cross, yet it cannot come to us in any other way than through the Word" (LC, V, 31). And the Sacrament is the Word in action, bringing us everything the Gospel Word offers.

And so the real presence of Christ's body and blood in the Sacrament and the divine blessings it brings are inextricably bound together. That is why Luther not only fought for the Real Presence but urged all penitent Christians to partake of the Sacrament often as the most comforting and concrete proof of God's love and forgiveness.

Today we can learn something from this emphasis in our Confessions. For more than two centuries now theologians and historians have by their studies tried to get back to the "historical Jesus," to become, as it were, a contemporary of His, like one of His disciples. Luther and our Confessions turn the whole order around. We do not through historical science or any other contorted method wend our way back to Jesus. He, the historical Jesus, the same one who died for us and rose again, the same Christ who was exalted and "will openly come again to judge the living and the dead" (AC, III, 6)—*He* comes to us in His Supper, becomes our contemporary, feeds us with His true body and blood, and bestows upon us here and now *all* He did for us as our Savior.

There is only one proper response to such a banquet. We are to come to it as often as it is celebrated, eat and drink His body and blood, and believe the promises, the stupendous promises summed up in that little phrase "for you" (SC, VI, 6-10). All this makes us worthy communicants, frequent communicants, happy communicants. Listen to Luther on this matter in his Large Catechism (V, 64-66):

A promise is attached to the commandment, as we heard above, which should most powerfully draw and impel us. Here stand the gracious and lovely words, "This is my body, given *for you*," "This is my blood, poured out *for you* for the

71

forgiveness of sins." These words, I have said, are not preached to wood or stone but to you and me; otherwise Christ might as well have kept quiet and not instituted a sacrament. Ponder, then, and include yourself personally in the "you" so that he may not speak to you in vain. In this sacrament he offers us all the treasure he brought from heaven. . . .

But what if we do not feel our need of the Sacrament? Again Luther has some good advice for us. He says: "At least believe the Scriptures. They will not lie to you, and they know your flesh better than you yourself do" (ibid., 76).

Before leaving the doctrine of the Lord's Supper we must mention a couple of points which are important and are still discussed today.

The Roman Church in Luther's day taught a doctrine called transubstantiation. This doctrine, developed in the early Middle Ages, affirmed that at the moment when the priest spoke the words of institution the bread and wine were *transformed* into the body and blood of Christ, although the appearance and taste of bread and wine remained. This transformation was permanent, so that after the celebration of the Sacrament the body and blood of Christ remained and could be worshiped by the people. All this was emphatically condemned as a "subtle sophistry" (SA, III, vi, 5; cf. FC Ep, VII, 22), for Paul teaches that the bread and wine remain in the Lord's Supper. The Lutherans also denied that "the visible forms of the blessed bread and wine are to be adored," although "Christ himself, true God and man, who is truly and essentially present in the Supper when it is rightly used, should be adored in spirit and in truth in all places but especially where his community is assembled" (FC SD, VII, 126).

Finally, what makes the Sacrament of the Altar what it is, a blessed means of salvation? It is "the whole action or administration of this sacrament (namely, that in a Christian assembly we take bread and wine, consecrate it, distribute it, receive it, eat and drink it, and therewith proclaim the Lord's death)" (ibid., 84). Essentially there are three things that make the Sacrament: the almighty words of institution, the distribution of the bread and wine, and the eating and drinking of the same. The concern of our Confessions is that the Sacrament be *used* often and properly; when this happens great blessings come to Christ's church.

# xv. Living the Christian Life

Church history is filled with tragic controversies and misunderstandings. Perhaps one of the most persistent misunderstandings of our Roman Catholic friends during the past 400 years of church history is that we Lutherans do not take good works seriously and urge them enough. The argument has often been advanced that the Lutheran insistence on salvation by grace alone and justification by faith in Christ alone indicates that good works have little value for Lutherans, for they cannot help to save us and make us right with God.

This was, and still today tragically is, a total misunderstanding of our Lutheran position and of our deepest convictions. More is written in our Confessions on the topic of good works and the Christian life than any other subject. One entire article in the Formula of Concord addresses itself exclusively to the necessity of good works, love, and obedience to God's law in the Christian's life. Luther's discussion of the Ten Commandments in his Large Catechism occupies more space than all the rest of the book combined. If one had any criticism of the Large Catechism, it would be that Luther did not devote more attention to the Creed, although his discussion of the Creed there is truly a masterpiece. Finally, Melanchthon in the Apology of the Augsburg Confession as he treats justification through faith spends more time speaking of love and good works and their relation to faith in the life of a Christian than of justification itself, which is the central article of our religion.

No Roman Catholic theologian ever spoke or wrote more emphatically, more clearly, more winsomely about sanctification and works of love than our Confessions. And no Roman Catholic theologian urged sanctification and good works and their value and how they please God more than Luther and our Confessions.

Just what do our Confessions say about the matter? As I

73

answer this question I will primarily follow Melanchthon's masterful discussion of the subject in the Apology (IV, 122-182).

He entitles this section "Love and the Keeping of the Law," and the great point he wishes to make is that love and good works follow and flow from faith (ibid., 111). "After we have been justified and regenerated by faith, therefore, we begin to fear and love God, to pray and expect help from him, to thank and praise him, and to submit to him in our afflictions. Then we also begin to love our neighbor because our hearts have spiritual and holy impulses" (ibid., 125, cf. 129). Melanchthon is saying that the Holy Spirit, when He through the Gospel creates faith in a person and justifies him, at the same time gives that person a new life, a life of love toward God and all men.

Without faith there can be no good works in God's eyes, no true obedience to the Law, although the unregenerated man can sometimes attain a high degree of "civil righteousness" (an outward adherence to the Commandments), which is highly commendable to the world within the sphere of civil and social action and can be very beneficial. But without faith it is impossible to love God. "How," Melanchthon asks, "can the human heart love God while it knows that in his terrible wrath he is overwhelming us with temporal and eternal calamities? The law always accuses us, it always shows that God is wrathful. We cannot love God until we have grasped his mercy by faith. Only then does he become an object that can be loved" (ibid., 128-129). I suppose such a statement would appear quite unrealistic and outlandish to many in our secular society today. The very idea of God's wrath seems completely remote in our materialistic age. But if one believes in a living God, and if one believes in the Law, one will understand that Melanchthon's position is correct, or the entire Christian religion is nonsense.

And so the Law can be kept only by Christians. This is exactly the conclusion of our Confessions. It sounds like an utterly untenable, yes arrogant, conclusion to the unbeliever. What difference is there whether an unbeliever or a Christian saves another's life or gives great sums to the poor? It is exactly the same good work in either case.

That is the way the world and all who do not know Christ assess the matter. And they are right within their own sphere of "civil righteousness." Who would not judge the righteousness of the Pharisee to be higher and greater than that of the publican in Christ's parable (Luke 18:9-14)?

But the matter is seen altogether differently in God's economy and judgment. Mere outward conformity to the Law does not impress Him; in fact, it does not even exist in this fallen eon, not even among Christians (FC SD, IV, 8).

God judges our actions, all of them, by the *context* in which they are done. God is pleased with our lives and our actions, not because we live up to the Law but because we are *"in Christ"* (Ap, IV, 140). This is an exceedingly difficult concept even for Christians to comprehend, because it is so utterly unexpected, so utterly evangelical. Melanchthon is not saying that our keeping the Law and pleasing God by our lives has nothing to do with the Ten Commandments—they remain the norm and God's immutable will for human action; but it is not the external doing itself that pleases God, but the doer. Listen to Melanchthon as he explains this doctrine: "The incipient [our imperfect beginning of] keeping of the law does not please God for its own sake, but for the sake of faith in Christ" (ibid., 166). Again he says: "Being reconciled by faith we are accounted righteous because of Christ, not because of the law or our works. The incipient keeping of the law pleases God because of faith; because of faith our failure to keep it is not imputed to us" (ibid., 177, cf. 172). Once again Melanchthon almost paradoxically says: "But a man keeps the law as soon as he hears that God is reconciled to us for Christ's sake even though we cannot satisfy the law. When faith takes hold of Christ, the mediator, the heart is at peace and begins to love God and to keep the law. It knows that now it is pleasing to God for the sake of Christ, the mediator, even though its incipient keeping of the law is impure and far from perfect" (ibid., 270, cf. 308-310, 359).

What a remarkable, encouraging, and comforting doctrine this is! All that I do is pleasing to God because I am *in Christ,* because I accept Him as my Savior and Mediator; whether I am a banker, or a pastor, or a secretary or nurse or housewife or little child, everything I do, everything, small and great— even though imperfect and tainted with sin and bad motives—everything pleases God! And all because I am in Christ, because I believe in Him with a faith and confidence wrought through the Gospel by the Holy Spirit alone. What a way to live! Knowing that whether I work or play, succeed or fail, God is pleased with me for Christ's sake, for His sake loves me and all I do.

Faith—or more precisely the Holy Spirit working in

believers—always, like a good tree, brings forth "good fruits" (AC, VI, 1). Faith and love must always be distinguished. We are justified alone by faith in Christ; love proceeds from faith and flows from it. But the two can never be separated. Where there is faith in Christ, love and good works always follow. They absolutely must and do follow. "It is impossible to separate faith from love for God, be it ever so small. For through Christ we come to the Father; and having received the forgiveness of sins, we become sure that we have a gracious God who cares about us, we call upon him, give thanks to him, fear and love him" (Ap, IV, 141). In fact, one of the very purposes of our being justified by faith is that we might love God and our neighbor and produce good works. Listen to Melanchthon as he emphasizes this fact: "We are justified for this very purpose, that, being righteous, we might begin to do good works and obey God's law. For this purpose we are reborn and receive the Holy Spirit, that this new life might have new works and new impulses, the fear and love of God, hatred of lust, etc." (ibid., 348-349). This is reminiscent of a very well known statement of Luther's on the power of Spirit-wrought faith. It is cited in the Formula of Concord (SD, IV, 10) and bears quotation (we used to memorize it when I was a seminarian):

> Faith is a divine work in us that transforms us and begets us anew from God, kills the Old Adam, makes us entirely different people in heart, spirit, mind, and all our powers, and brings the Holy Spirit with it. Oh, faith is a living, busy, active, mighty thing, so that it is impossible for it not to be constantly doing what is good. Likewise, faith does not ask if good works are to be done, but before one can ask, faith has already done them and is constantly active. Whoever does not perform such good works is a faithless man, blindly tapping around in search of faith and good works without knowing what either faith or good works are, and in the meantime he chatters and jabbers a great deal about faith and good works. Faith is a vital, deliberate trust in God's grace, so certain that it would die a thousand times for it. And such confidence and knowledge of divine grace makes us joyous, mettlesome, and merry toward God and all creatures. This the Holy Spirit works by faith, and therefore without any coercion a man is willing and desirous to do good to everyone, to serve everyone, to suffer everything for the love of God and to his glory, who has been so gracious to him. It is therefore as impossible to separate works from faith as it is to separate heat and light from fire.

Luther's classic statement is reminiscent of a stanza from his favorite hymn, Paul Speratus' "Salvation unto Us Has Come":

> Faith clings to Jesus' cross alone
> And rests in Him unceasing;
> And by its fruits true faith is known,
> With love and hope increasing.
> Yet faith alone doth justify,
> Works serve thy neighbor and supply
> The proof that faith is living.

This joyous doctrine that our Christian lives are pleasing to God for Christ's sake does not imply that our fulfilling of the Law is ever sufficient, that we become perfect and need not repent. Quite the contrary! The Christian repents daily. "This faith arises in penitence," Melanchthon says (Ap, IV, 353). Should the Holy Spirit depart from us, we could not please God with a single thing we do (Ap, IV, 34, 35, 126, 132, 133, 135). Although we cooperate in our sanctification and do good works with a glad heart, it is the Spirit who alone works all good in us (FC SD, II, 65-66). Our sanctification is exclusively His work through the Word, just as is our conversion and faith in Christ (ibid., 26, 39). "Holy Scriptures ascribe conversion, faith in Christ, regeneration, renewal [sanctification], and everything that belongs to its real beginning and completion . . . altogether and alone to the divine operation of the Holy Spirit" (ibid., 25).

Yes, we need the Holy Spirit daily to live the Christian life. And we need Christ our Mediator to plead for us daily; for our righteousness before God, the righteousness that avails and counts before Him, is always Christ's righteousness (Ap, IV, 162-163), never our own imperfect efforts.

And so the Christian life is a struggle: a struggle against sin which never ceases, and a struggle to please God with our lives. But a joyous struggle! For our sins are for Christ's sake not counted against us, and all our efforts, imperfect as they always are, are pleasing to our gracious and loving God.

# XVI. Church and State and Social Action

A great deal of literature has been written during our American Bicentennial about the relation between church and state, and most Americans would no doubt conclude that our American Constitution arranged things very well indeed. Of course, there was never any total separation between church and state in our country; for the interests and spheres of church and state often overlap, for instances, in areas touching on education, ethics, injustice, and social action. But each has its own sphere of activity, according to our founding fathers, and there ought to be as little encroachment on the sphere of the other as possible.

I wonder how many Lutherans realize that long before John Locke, the great English philosopher whose ideas about human rights and government were embodied by our founding fathers (John Adams, Thomas Jefferson, and others) in formulating the philosophy underlying our Constitution, Luther and our Lutheran Confessions had said much the same thing about the relation between church and state.

In two different sections in the Augsburg Confession and the Apology Melanchthon discusses these crucial issues. Remember, he was living in an age when absolute monarchs ruled the great nations of the Christian world. Representative government as we know it today was virtually unheard-of. And the papacy claimed to have absolute authority even in the civil realm over all earthly rulers. His ideas, therefore, about a balance between civil and ecclesiastical authority were bound to offend both sides. Humanly speaking, there was very little possibility that such ideas would gain general acceptance. But he addressed himself to them nevertheless, for Scripture says a great deal about the church and the state.

The *first principle* our Confessions lay down (AC, XVI, 1-2) is that civil government, with all its faults and imperfections, is "instituted and ordained by God." Therefore Christians are encouraged to occupy civil offices, serve as princes and judges, pass laws and sentences, and in their civil capacity punish criminals and evildoers. They can buy and sell, take oaths when required by civil authorities, and serve as soldiers and fight for their country.

What ruler or magistrate would not appreciate Lutherans as his subjects? One of my professors used to say that Lutherans are the best citizens a country has; for they love and respect their nation as instituted by God, and they actively and willingly serve their country.

Or at least they ought to, according to our Lutheran Confessions. Here is the blueprint for good citizenship, social concern, the right kind of social activism: each Christian, recognizing the divine institution of his country, and according to his calling (SC, IV, 1-15), doing everything he can for the common good. No Christian has any right to forsake his country in any of the duties mentioned above.

It is significant that our Confessions maintain that the Christian *citizen* carries out his obligations to the nation and society. Never do our Confessions say that such is the obligation of the church. And this leads to the *second principle* enunciated by Melanchthon.

This principle is simply that the church has certain powers, responsibilities, and obligations; and so does the state. The two ought not be confused. Sometimes, as I mentioned before, there are overlapping concerns. But the principle remains and should be observed as closely as possible. Melanchthon's statement (AC, XXVIII, 5, 11-18; cf. Ap, XVI, 3-8) on the distinction between the two powers is a classic and ought to be quoted extensively:

> Our teachers assert that according to the Gospel the power of keys or the power of bishops is a power and command of God to preach the Gospel, to forgive and retain sins, and to distribute the sacraments. . . . Temporal authority is concerned with matters altogether different from the Gospel. Temporal power does not protect the soul, but with the sword and physical penalties it protects body and goods from the power of others.
>
> Therefore, the two authorities, the spiritual and the temporal, are not to be mingled or confused, for the spiritual power has its commission to preach the Gospel and ad-

minister the sacraments. Hence it should not invade the function of the other, should not set up and depose kings, should not annul temporal laws or undermine obedience to government, should not make or prescribe to the temporal power laws concerning worldly matters. Christ himself said, "My kingship is not of this world," and again, "Who made me a judge or divider over you?" Paul also wrote in Phil. 3:20, "Our commonwealth is in heaven," and in II Cor. 10:4, 5, "The weapons of our warfare are not worldly but have divine power to destroy strongholds and every proud obstacle to the knowledge of God."

Thus our teachers distinguish the two authorities and the functions of the two powers, directing that both be held in honor as the highest gifts of God on earth.

These significant statements from our Confessions do not teach an *absolute* separation of church and state as Anabaptists and other sects taught during the time of the Reformation. The established church in Saxony and many other parts of Germany and in other Lutheran countries was Lutheran. But this statement of Melanchthon's, which sounds so surprisingly modern, stands as a milestone in the history of Christian thought. After 450 years, years often of frustration and failure, it still remains the best formula for the proper relation between church and state, for good and enlightened citizenship, and for effective and intelligent social action by Christians living in a secular society.

# XVII. Predestination and the Election of Grace

The reader might ask, why a chapter on such a subject in a little summary volume like this? Are there no more important things in our Confessions to write about?

I think I can justify writing about predestination for two reasons. *First,* our Formula of Concord devotes a great deal of discussion to the subject, even though there was no real controversy among Lutherans on the matter at that time. *Second,* and more important, God's predestination of all His children, His eternal election of grace, is revealed in Scripture and presented in our Confessions not to confuse or disturb Christians or to stir up needless and sinful speculation but to comfort Christians and deepen their appreciation of God's almighty grace in Christ.

Luther once said that predestination is strong wine that ought not be given to children. He meant that Christians ought not speculate about the subject and try to pry out the inscrutable and hidden purposes of God. Rather Christians ought to view God's predestination in its proper context, as something that *adds* to the comfort of the Gospel. This is exactly the way our Formula of Concord presents the matter. After one knows what Christ has done to redeem the human race, after one has accepted the benefits of Christ offered by the Spirit through the Word and sacraments, after one knows he has been justified and made a child of God through faith in Christ, after one is assured that the Holy Spirit will graciously keep him in that faith—then, then the doctrine of predestination is presented to give him even greater certainty and assurance of God's grace (FC SD, XI, 14-23).

And that is just what predestination is: an election of grace, God's loving and gracious purpose from eternity to bring to faith and save us who are His children (ibid., 24). Predestination is an eternal decree which is utterly certain and cannot be thwarted. A Christian can fall from grace (ibid., 42), also the elect, but God will graciously again restore His elect (ibid., 75). One of my former professors put the doctrine of the Formula of Concord very simply in a way I think any child can understand: Predestination simply means that everything God has done in time to save us and make us His children and preserve us in the faith, He determined in Christ to do for us in eternity. So my salvation is not the result of any whimsical actions or reactions of God, but of His eternal purpose for me.

That ought to afford me certainty and comfort. And that is exactly what our Formula of Concord (ibid., 45-47) wants to provide for us:

> This doctrine also affords the beautiful and glorious comfort that God was so deeply concerned about every individual Christian's conversion, righteousness, and salvation and so faithfully minded about it that "even before the foundation of the world was laid" he held counsel and ordained "according to his purpose" [Eph. 1:4; 2 Tim. 1:9] how he would bring me thereto and keep me therein. Furthermore, God wanted to insure my salvation so firmly and certainly—for due to the weakness and wickedness of our flesh it could easily slip from our fingers, and through the deceit and power of the devil and the world it could easily be snatched and taken from our hands—that he ordained my salvation in his eternal purpose, which cannot fail or be overthrown, and put it for safekeeping into the almighty hand of our Savior, Jesus Christ, out of which no one can pluck us (John 10:28). For this reason, too, Paul asks, Since we are called according to the purpose of God, "who will separate us from the love of God in Christ?" (Rom. 8:35).

There is a mystery in our predestination. It appears to us in Scripture and our Confessions like a coin with only one side. For God's election and predestination pertains only to us who are Christians, not to all people (ibid., 23). Yet there is no predestination to damnation (ibid., 7, 41, 80). Rather, God earnestly desires to save all (ibid., 28), and His Gospel invitation to all sinners is always serious (ibid., 34, 68).

In the face of this mystery we do not complain that God has not chosen all, nor do we ask why. We simply praise God for choosing us, and thank Him for His grace.

A few years ago I preached in chapel at Concordia Seminary in St. Louis on Rom. 8:28, which deals with eternal election. Dr. Spitz, one of my older colleagues, came to me afterwards and said it was the first time he had heard a sermon in chapel on the subject. I think he appreciated it. And why not? As our Confessions say (ibid., 48-49), this doctrine gives us

> the glorious comfort, in times of trial and affliction, that in his counsel before the foundation of the world God has determined and decreed that he will assist us in all our necessities, grant us patience, give us comfort, create hope, and bring everything to such an issue that we shall be saved. Again, Paul presents this in a most comforting manner when he points out that before the world began God ordained in his counsel through which specific cross and affliction he would conform each of his elect to "the image of his Son," and that in each case the afflictions should and must "work together for good" since they are "called according to his purpose." From this Paul draws the certain and indubitable conclusion that neither "tribulation nor anguish, neither death nor life, etc. can separate us from the love of God in Christ Jesus" (Rom. 8:28, 29, 35, 38, 39).

# XVIII. The End of the Road— Eternal Life

"If a man die, shall he live again?" (Job 14:14). This is certainly one of the profoundest questions that can occupy anyone's mind. For if we cannot believe in eternal life, we cannot really believe in God at all. Job in all his consternation and suffering knew that. If there is no eternal life, no eschatology, i. e., nothing happening at the end of the world and the end of our lives, then all we have been saying about God, and creation, and sin and grace, and Christ and atonement, and all the rest have no meaning at all.

Our age has great trouble with the doctrine of eternal life. I once knew a man who confessed faith in the Trinity but doubted whether there was any existence beyond the grave. What utter confusion! But worse, theologians today are professing elaborate doctrinal positions which claim that heaven and salvation are here and now, and beyond this life the future holds nothing for us. To which Paul replies: "If in this life only we have hope in Christ, we are of all men most miserable" (1 Cor. 15:19). Somewhere I once read that fully one sixth of the New Testament speaks of what is yet to come for Christians: Christ's return in glory, the resurrection of the dead, the final judgment, and then eternal glory.

It might seem strange then that our Lutheran Confessions do not devote more space to the subject of eschatology and eternal life. There is only a brief article on the subject of Christ's return to judgment in the Augsburg Confession (AC, XVII). And this article merely sums up what was already said in the ancient creeds.

But really our Confessions are permeated with the firm and anxious anticipation of the return of Christ and with confidence in the life to come (e. g., SA, II, iv, 15). The subscribers of the *Book of Concord* preface their confession with this future hope: "By the help of God's grace we, too, intend to persist in this confession until our blessed end and to appear before the judgment seat of our Lord Jesus Christ with joyful and fearless hearts and consciences" (Preface to the *Book of Concord,* p. 9; cf. Preface to the Apology, 19). All confession is made and all work is carried out in anticipation of Christ's return and the glory that will follow (FC SD, XII, 40). Such is the certainty of the victory and salvation which will accompany Christ as He returns in glory.

Of course, there was secularism and even practical atheism in Luther's day. But the Confessions reflect a conviction, strange to our day, that we live in the last times. All the signs of the end are revealed, and our life and activities are now directed toward that imminent end. Meanwhile, by faith's anticipation we have eternal life now. "The Gospel brings not the shadow of eternal things but the eternal blessings themselves" (Ap, VII, 15). "The Gospel . . . is the forgiveness of sins and the beginning of eternal life in the hearts of believers" (Ap, XVI, 6). Our regeneration by the Spirit and our faith in Christ make us heirs and partakers of that eternal life now—rather these are "the beginning of eternal life" (Ap, IV, 352; VII, 15; LC, III, 54).

Whenever salvation is mentioned in our Confessions, eternal life is the goal of it all (LC, IV, 25). And so it is also with the central article of justification. "Just as justification belongs to faith, so eternal life belongs to it" (Ap, IV, 354).

Our Confessions teach a very uncomplicated and ingenuous Biblical eschatology (i. e., doctrine of the last things). They reject all speculations about a rapture, a thousand years' reign of Christ on earth before the end, a universal conversion of the Jews (AC, XVII, 5), opinions almost as common then as in our day. The Book of Revelation, which was recognized as apocalyptic in form and therefore highly figurative as it depicts future events such as Christ's return and eternal life, was interpreted by the Lutherans in the light of the straightforward teachings of the rest of the New Testament, not vice versa.

To the Lutheran Confessions the future of history and all things is simple and clear. Christ will return suddenly and unexpectedly and soon. All the dead will rise; all the living and dead will be judged by Christ, and those who believe in Him will be saved forever. The earth and creation as we know it will be destroyed, and a "new heaven and earth" will be created. And then—heaven with God and the Lamb! Because that is heaven: to be with God in His glory.

How all this will be we do not know yet. To the Lutheran reformers the anticipation of it all was so overwhelming that speculation on the when and how of it was simply crowded out of their theology and expectations. "Eye hath not seen, nor ear heard, neither have entered into the heart of man, the things which God hath prepared for them that love Him" (1 Cor. 2:9).

Such a futuristic view will seem naive to both our secularist friends today, who have no hope, and also to our fundamentalist friends with their intricate and ever-changing millennialistic and dispensationalistic themes. But this was the belief, confession, and hope of the Lutherans in the 16th century. Here were forward-looking people, triumphant Christians, who were happy on earth and knew they would be blessed in heaven. We who today call ourselves Lutherans can do no better than to recapture such a confidence and heavenly viewpoint.

And so we have arrived at the end of this chapter and the end of this little book. And I can think of no more appropriate closing than the words of Luther in his explanation to the Seventh Petition (SC, III, 20):

> We pray in this petition, as in a summary, that our Father in heaven may deliver us from all manner of evil, whether it affect body or soul, property or reputation, and that at last, when the hour of death comes, he may grant us a blessed end and graciously take us from this world of sorrow to himself in heaven.

*Soli Deo gloria*—to God alone the glory!

# Glossary

*Communion of Natures*—The divine and human natures of Christ, since the Personal Union, are in communion with each other and never separated from each other, although each retains its own essential properties (FC Ep, VIII, 6-18).

*Concupiscence*—Lust; the innate depravity inherited from our first parents, whereby all are habitually inclined to evil (AC, II, 1-2). This is a living power from which all sins proceed (Ap, II, 3, 6, 7).

*Confession*—A jointly held formal statement of faith, similar to a creed. When in this book we speak of the "Lutheran Confessions" or just the "Confessions," we mean the writings included in the *Book of Concord* of 1580.

*Contrition*—Sorrow over sin; terrors of conscience because of our guilt before God.

*Conversion*—See Repentance; the work of the Holy Spirit in bringing a sinner to see his sin through the Law and to believe in Christ through the Gospel.

*Creed*—A statement of faith.

*Doctrine*—Teaching.

*Election*—See Predestination.

*Enthusiasm*—The heresy that the Holy Spirit comes with grace and salvation to sinners without the external means of the Scriptures, the spoken Word of the Gospel, and the sacraments (SA, III, viii).

*Evangelical*—Gospel-centered, Gospel-oriented.

*Excommunication*—The exclusion of hardened and impenitent sinners from the Christian community, retaining their sins, depriving them of the Sacrament of the Altar until they repent (Tr, 60).

*Exegesis*—The interpreting or exposition of the Scriptures.

*Faith*—Trust in Christ; receiving Christ and His atoning work; knowledge of Christ and His benefits (His work of salvation).

*Freedom of the Will*—Since the Fall man is not only sinful and guilty before God, but he is a slave of sin and unable to come to God, to obey His law or believe in Him. Only the Spirit of God through Baptism and the Gospel can quicken and regenerate him. The unregenerated person has no freedom of will to serve God or come to Him.

*Good Works*—See Righteousness (No. 4: Righteousness of Believers); works done by believers in Christ according to God's law, empowered by the Holy Spirit (AC, XX, 29).

*Gospel*—The good news that God has saved us by sending Christ to obey God's law and to suffer the punishment for all our sins in our stead. (Often our Confessions use the term "Gospel" simply to denote Scripture, or the entire teaching of Scripture, or one of the books written by the New Testament evangelists.)

*Grace*—God's undeserved love toward lost sinners. This grace is not some quiescent love which does nothing, but is action that centers in God sending His Son to save us and His Holy Spirit to bring us to faith in Christ and to sanctify and save us.

*Impute*—To reckon. God reckons to us who believe in Christ the righteousness Christ accomplished by His obedience to the divine law and by His innocent and sacrificial death (Ap, IV, 230, 221).

*Incarnation*—Called also Personal Union; the doctrine that the Son of God, who existed from eternity, became man, assumed a human nature consisting of body and soul, in order to save fallen mankind. Christ remains one Person, true God and true man into all eternity (FC Ep, VIII, 5).

*Justification*—God's counting lost and guilty sinners righteous because of Christ's atoning work.

*Law*—The immutable will of God, showing man how he should behave in thought, word, and deed (FC SD, V, 17; VI, 15).

*Mediator*—Christ is our Mediator, or Advocate, who pleads our cause before God, and this He does because of His sacrificial and atoning work (Ap, IV, 214-215).

*Merit*—A non-Biblical word used throughout the Confessions in two very different ways: 1. To denote man's attempt (usually under the papacy) to earn forgiveness or years off purgatory or eternal life from God; 2. To denote all that Christ did to save us, His obedience under the Law and His atoning death as our Substitute.

*Ministry*—The work of the Holy Spirit through the Gospel Word and the sacraments to convey God's grace, bring sinners to faith, and sustain that faith (AC, V, 1-2). Sometimes the term is used for the office of the pastor or minister (Tr, 67).

*Monergism*—The doctrine that man's conversion is alone the work of the Holy Spirit through the Gospel, or means of grace (FC, II).

*Obedience*—A Biblical (Rom. 5:19) and confessional term (FC, III, 12, 15, 32) indicating the saving work of Christ's obedience to the divine law and His suffering and dying, which is all imputed to the believer. See Righteousness (No. 2: Righteousness of Christ).

*Office of the Keys*—The power given the entire church to forgive and retain sins by the power of the Gospel and the Law (SA, III, vii, 1).

*Original Sin*—The corruption of human nature brought about

through Adam's fall and transmitted to all humans through propagation (AC, II, 1-2). It consists of a total lack of fear and love toward God and of concupiscence (Ap, II, 3).

*Penance*—The Roman Catholic perversion of repentance, which was called a sacrament and consisted of contrition, confession to a priest, and satisfaction (human works which merit God's forgiveness) (Ap, XII, 8-16).

*Personal Union*—See Incarnation.

*Predestination*—God's determination from eternity, or God's eternal election of grace, to bring to faith and save eternally those individuals who believe in Christ to the end. Predestination pertains only to the children of God. It is immutable. There is no predestination to damnation.

*Propitiation*—Christ's work of satisfying the wrath of God the Father by His perfect obedience to the divine law and His innocent death as our Substitute (Ap, IV, 212, 214).

*Regeneration*—Spiritual rebirth, worked by the Holy Spirit through Baptism or later in life through the power of the Gospel, consisting of the bestowal of faith in Christ (AC, V).

*Renewal*—Sanctification (see definition below), worked by the Holy Spirit in those who are born anew.

*Repentance*—Contrition plus faith; turning away from sin and turning to Christ, the Savior of sinners.

*Righteousness*—1. Righteousness of Faith—God counts us just or righteous only for Christ's sake (because of His atoning work or righteousness), through faith in Christ.

2. Righteousness of Christ (often called a "foreign righteousness" because we do not perform it)—His perfect obedience to the Law and sacrificial and innocent death in our place, all of which is reckoned to the sinner who believes the Gospel.

3. Civil Righteousness—the external obedience to civil or natural law which to a degree can be achieved by unbelievers but does not avail before God.

4. Righteousness of Believers—the new obedience to the Law worked by the Holy Spirit in those whom He has converted through the Gospel and to whom He has given faith in Christ (FC SD, III, 30).

*Sanctification*—The new life a person lives when he believes in Christ. In this new life the Holy Spirit leads him to obey the Law for Christ's sake.

*Sola Fide*—"By faith alone"; the phrase used to affirm that a lost sinner is justified alone by faith in Christ, his Propitiator and Savior.

*Sola Gratia*—"By grace alone"; the phrase used to affirm that poor sinners are saved eternally by grace alone without any contribution or good works on their part.

*Sola Scriptura*—"Scripture alone"; the phrase used to show that all Christian doctrine is drawn from the Scriptures and that all teachers and teachings are judged by them.

*Symbol*—A confession with which Christians identify and around which they rally, like a flag. The word is used synonymously with the word "confession."

*Synergism*—The heresy that a sinner cooperates with the Holy Spirit in his conversion (FC, II).

*Theology*—Language about God; doctrine.

*Transubstantiation*—The Roman Catholic doctrine of the Lord's Supper, rejected by the Confessions, that the bread and wine in the Sacrament lose their substance and are transformed into the body and blood of Christ in such a way that bread and wine are no longer present (FC Ep, VII, 22).

*Trinity*—The classical Christian doctrine that one God, or divine essence, consists of three distinct Persons, Father, Son, and Holy Spirit.

# Questions

## INTRODUCTION

1. Why ought Lutheran lay people today study the Lutheran Confessions?
2. What are the advantages of having a definite number of Confessions?
3. What are the advantages of our *Book of Concord* containing creeds and Confessions written at different times and from different perspectives?

## I. THE LUTHERAN CONFESSIONS: WHAT ARE THEY?

1. Can and ought a Christian be sure of his doctrine? Why is doctrine important?
2. Do you think the Lutheran Church is right in requiring its pastors to subscribe unconditionally to its Confessions? Why or why not?
3. Do you think we need new, up-to-date Confessions today? or perhaps additional ones to meet modern problems? Why or why not?

## II. THE LUTHERAN CONFESSIONS AND THE BIBLE

1. Find evidence from the Bible for the *sola Scriptura* principle.
2. What are several "isms" today which challenge this principle?
3. Could confessionalism, or loyalty to the Lutheran Confessions, threaten one's faithfulness to Scripture? If so, how?

## III. THE LUTHERAN CONFESSIONS AND THE GOSPEL

1. Why is it important that our Confessions are Gospel-centered?
2. List some "false gospels" of the past and present that are opposed to our Confessions.

## IV. THE HOLY GOSPEL AND THE HOLY SCRIPTURES

1. State as many differences and similarities as you can between the Scriptures and the Gospel.
2. Why do you think some people today want to make the Gospel a norm for doctrine, and not Scripture? Why is this harmful?
3. What is the proper relationship between Scripture and the Gospel?

## V. WHO IS GOD?

1. Why can we not define God? What would happen if we did try to define Him?
2. What would be the consequences of denying the Trinity?
3. Why is the doctrine of the Trinity so difficult to "believe"?
4. Why is it so important not only to know who God is but what He has done?


## VI. THE MARVELS OF GOD'S CREATION

1. Why do you think our Confessions dwell more on God's continuing creation than on His first creation of all things in six days?
2. Name some false ideas about the doctrine of creation that are held in our day.
3. How does the doctrine of creation bear on our teaching of the Gospel today?
4. What evidence do you find that people today often deny God's existence in practice even though they do not come right out and say so?


## VII. HOW MAN RUINED GOD'S CREATION

1. Why do you think our Confessions speak more about original sin than about actual sins?
2. Identify references to original sin in sermons you hear (in church, on radio or TV). Do pastors preach too much or too little on this doctrine?
3. Why should a Christian know he is a sinner?


## VIII. WHO IS JESUS CHRIST AND WHAT HAS HE DONE?

1. What has the Incarnation to do with the world today?
2. Why is it necessary that the attributes of the Godhead (divine nature) be communicated to the human nature of Jesus?
3. List some great "salvation" themes in our Confessions and find their basis in Scripture.
4. Show how these themes are still relevant as we witness to Christ today.
5. Do you think it is important to emphasize the wrath of God today? What does such an emphasis have to do with being evangelical?
6. What inadequate views of Christ are held by many people today? What is wrong with these ideas about Him?


## IX. THE CENTER OF IT ALL: JUSTIFICATION BY FAITH

1. Melanchthon says that justification is a "judicial" action of God. Show how this might be made relevant in our day.
2. Why do you think the article of justification was thought to be the central article of the faith by the reformers? Can we still say this?
3. List some false ideas concerning faith which would undermine the doctrine of justification.
4. Discuss what it means to be justified *by faith* and how important it is that we are justified by faith *alone*.

## X. THE WORK OF THE SPIRIT

1. Do you agree with the criticism that Lutherans do not sufficiently emphasize the work of the Holy Spirit? If so, what do you think is the reason for this situation?
2. List and discuss several things the Holy Spirit has done and still does for us.
3. List and discuss some current misunderstandings about the Holy Spirit's work.
4. Why is it so significant for the church today to know that the "ministry" belongs to the Holy Spirit and His ministry is to witness to Christ?

## XI. THE CHURCH AND ITS PASTORS

1. In what ways is the Lutheran doctrine of the church and its "marks" Gospel-centered?
2. Why should Christians love and honor their pastors?
3. List as many qualifications and duties of a pastor as you can, and arrange them in order of importance.
4. What changes, if any, do you think we should make in our method of calling pastors and teachers?

## XII. THE WORK OF THE LAW AND THE GOSPEL: REPENTANCE

1. List a number of differences between the Law and the Gospel.
2. Discuss ways in which people commonly confuse Law and Gospel.
3. When should the Law be used, and when the Gospel?
4. How could pastors and lay people urge repentance more effectively today?

## XIII. BAPTISM

1. What did Luther mean when he said we should "use" our baptism? How can we do this to a greater extent in our daily life?
2. What is the importance of infant baptism? Why have we Lutherans been unsuccessful in persuading so many of our Protestant friends to see its value and necessity?
3. Why ought we to hold to infant faith and teach it more?

## XIV. THE LORD'S SUPPER

1. What reasons do some Christians give for rejecting the real presence of Christ's body and blood in the Lord's Supper?
2. Why do Lutherans not attend the Lord's Supper more often when it affords such great blessings? How would you encourage people to attend more regularly?
3. Why is it important to recognize that the Lord's Supper is a means of grace?

## XV. LIVING THE CHRISTIAN LIFE

1. Does the belief that the Holy Spirit works all good within us discourage good works? Why or why not?
2. What are the reasons Christians strive to do good works?
3. Discuss the doctrine that God is pleased with all that we do for Christ's sake. What are the implications of this for living a sanctified life?
4. Do good works help to preserve faith? Why or why not?

## XVI. CHURCH AND STATE AND SOCIAL ACTION

1. Does Christianity or Lutheranism prescribe any special kind of government or political structure? Discuss.
2. Is the church as such to engage in any kind of social action? If so, what kind, and in what way?
3. Discuss the apparently presumptuous statement: "A Lutheran is the best kind of citizen."
4. List in two columns the functions of the church and those of civil government. How do these functions overlap in our modern society?

## XVII. PREDESTINATION AND THE ELECTION OF GRACE

1. How would you talk about election to an unbeliever?
2. If a Christian asked you why all people weren't saved, how would you reply?
3. Try to present all the comforts in the doctrine of predestination and election.

## XVIII. THE END OF THE ROAD—ETERNAL LIFE

1. Discuss the reasons for modern secularism.
2. If you found a person who did not believe in eternal life, how would you react and what would you say to him/her?
3. Why do our Confessions reject millennialism (1,000-year reign, rapture, etc.)? What harm can there be in such speculations?
4. There are many sects and cults today that believe in some kind of "life after death" but not in Christ. What should the church's message be to them?
5. What does it mean to you to believe in eternal life?